THE
DONCASTER
ROVERS
MISCELLANY

ROBERT MARSHALL

The History Press

First published 2011

The History Press
The Mill, Brimscombe Port
Stroud, Gloucestershire, GL5 2QG
www.thehistorypress.co.uk

British Library Cataloguing in Publication Data.
A catalogue record for this book is available from the British Library.

ISBN 978 0 7524 5847 2

Typesetting and origination by The History Press
Printed in the EU for the History Press.

FOREWORD
by Laurie Sheffield

To be honest, I was not particularly excited when Rovers first came in to sign me. They were a side in the same division as my club, Newport County, and the move did not instantly appear much of a progression. That said, though, I was aware of the quality of players already at Doncaster and the club had a nice feeling about it, which was felt among all the players at that time. I knew straight away that it was the right move and I quickly settled in South Yorkshire – I loved the type of people in Doncaster and the town quickly became home. I would regularly go out before games to find people shouting messages of support, offering gifts of fruit from the market stalls, and I often returned home with armfuls of apples and bananas.

I was fortunate enough to play in a hugely talented and successful team which won the Division Four championship in 1966. We were together as a group both on and off the pitch, we would all work hard for each other on a Saturday afternoon then we'd all be out on a Saturday night together. That kind of atmosphere created a huge unity, which contributed significantly to our successes on the pitch. I felt that bond most keenly with my strike partner and great friend, Alick Jeffrey. We got on incredibly well, even 40 years later we were still going on holiday together.

Alick was simply a brilliant footballer, but I was also ideal for his game. All the other teams focused on how to stop Alick, they used to try to rough him up and use physical tactics but that was my job for Doncaster Rovers. I was strong and fit and I could stop the centre-halves from doing their job – I used to cause problems for them and Alick dropped off and made great use of the room I had created. It worked for us and we scored many, many goals together.

I remember Alick never liked training but he was such a character he always seemed to get away with it. If we were up against two good centre-backs and weren't getting any joy, I used to work the channels. I'd go to chase the full-back's ball down the wing and I'd pass Alick on the way. He'd be blowing hard, cheeks puffed out trying to catch his breath. I'd be chasing all over the pitch then all of a sudden Alick would get the ball 30 yards out and smash it into the top corner of the goal, then he'd come over to me and say 'I don't like doing all that running Laurie!'

My job throughout my career was to put people under pressure and to score goals. They used to give me the number nine shirt and that shirt was for one thing only. I loved to watch good players play good football in midfield but I was there for one reason, to score goals.

I am delighted to be invited down to every match at the Keepmoat Stadium and I have been thrilled with the recent success. The club still look after me and I am happy to do as much as I can with sponsors and supporters' groups in return.

I played for a number of clubs all around the country and enjoyed a very fruitful career, but Doncaster and my time with the Rovers was, without a shadow of a doubt, the best.

Laurie Sheffield, 2011

INTRODUCTION

In May 2003, Rovers winger Fran Tierney scored a goal that was golden in every sense imaginable. It was the goal which won the Conference play-off final and sent Doncaster Rovers back into the Football League, marking a new chapter in the history of the club and a return from the darkest days it has ever endured.

Since its birth in 1879, never has the club had its very existence threatened in such as way as befell it during the mid-1990s. Owner Ken Richardson's attempt to strip the life from the club, centring on the site on which its Belle Vue home stood, was littered with controversy and deceit. An attempt to sell Belle Vue, despite the fact it was owned by the council, was quickly followed by an arson attack on the Main Stand and then, with the likelihood of any financial gain drifting from view, a seemingly unwavering desire to see the club fall into extinction followed. The club endured a season like no other in 1997/98, finishing 92nd in a league structure made up of ninety-two clubs; they were finally cut adrift of the Football League with the ink dry on what appeared to be the final chapter of a story that had been over 100 years in the making.

The club had enjoyed better times along the way, flirting with Football League membership at the turn of the twentieth century, breaking records (which have still to be bettered) during the 1946/47 scason in winning the Third Division North title and enjoying a stint in English football's second tier throughout the 1950s under the forward-thinking tutelage of a once-supreme footballer in Peter Doherty, with a host of talented footballers. The club enjoyed FA Cup runs which delighted packed Belle Vue audiences who regularly numbered above 20,000.

The club battled to recapture these former glories throughout the next three decades, tantalisingly brushing with better days with names like Kitchen, O'Callaghan and Miller still providing much to cheer. The great Billy Bremner arrived to punch some passion back into the club during the late 1980s before almost strangling financial constraints led to the involvement of Richardson (later found guilty and imprisoned for the arson attack on Belle Vue) and his subsequent criminal decline of the club. The funeral of the club was held at the final game of that disastrous year in 1998 but the party after the wake was hosted by John Ryan, who managed to acquire the club shortly afterwards and restore life back through its tired and bruised exterior.

That goal in Stoke in 2003 marked the return of Doncaster Rovers and the celebrations that day were made all the more sweet because of all the heartache that had gone before. The club has continued to go from strength to strength, winning the Third Division the following year, the Football League Trophy, then the sweetest of days at Wembley before becoming established as a Championship side of real quality. It is safe to say that Rovers fans have never had it so good, but there are still a great many things that I look back on, good and bad, with great fondness and a smile.

Robert Marshall, 2011

HONOURS

Football League:
Division 2 Best season: 7th, 1901/02
Division 3 Champions: 2003/04
Division 3 (N) Champions: 1934/35, 1946/47, 1949/50
Division 4 Champions 1965/66, 1968/69

Runners-Up:
Division 3 (N): 1937/38, 1938/39
Division 4: 1983/84. Promoted 1980/81 (3rd)

League One play-off final winners: 2008

Football Conference play-off final winners: 2003

FA Cup: Best season: fifth round: 1952, 1954, 1955, 1956

Football League Cup: Best season: fifth round: 1976

Johnstone's Paint Trophy: winners 2007

Conference Trophy: winners 1999, 2000

Sheffield County Cup: winners 1891, 1912, 1936, 1938,
    1956, 1968, 1976, 1986

Midlands Counties League: Champions 1897, 1899

Sheffield & Hallamshire Senior Cup: winners 2001, 2002

Yorkshire Electricity Cup: winners 1995/96

STATS

Record Attendance: 37,149 v Hull City

Rovers' record attendance came in 1948 in a Division Three North game at Belle Vue when they played host to Hull City on 2 October in a match which attracted 37,149 spectators and ended 0–0. The club's record attendance since the move to the new Keepmoat Stadium came on 1 April 2008 as 15,001 watched the League One game against Leeds United.

Record Victory: 10–0 v Darlington

The Rovers' record league victory came on 25 January 1964 in a Division Four match against Darlington. They actually enjoyed a number of high-scoring games against the 'Quakers' throughout the 1960s but this was by far the most one-sided. The Rovers scorers that day were Hale (4), Booth (2), Ripley (2), Windross and Broadbent.

Record Defeat: 12–0 v Small Heath

The club's record defeat was at the hands of Small Heath in a Second Division game on 11 April 1903 when the club, still in its infancy, were beaten 12–0.

Highest League Scorer in Season: Clarrie Jordan, 42

Clarrie Jordan scored the club's record number of league goals in one season. The forward found the back of the net 42 times during the record-breaking season in 1946/47. His incredible personal goal tally led the side to the Division Three North league title.

Most Goals in a Game: Tom Keetley, 6

The most goals scored by a Rovers player in one match came during the 1928/29 season; Tom Keetley scored 6 of the Rovers' goals in the thrilling 7–4 win at Ashington.

Most Capped Player

Len Graham is the club's most capped player, winning 14 caps for Northern Ireland while with Rovers.

Record Appearances

Fred Emery is the club's record appearance holder making 417 outings in the league for Doncaster between 1924 and 1928. He played in an additional 20 FA Cup matches during his Rovers career, just ahead of Colin Douglas – fans' favourite 'Duggie' made 404 league appearances for the club in two spells between 1981 and 1993.

Youngest Player

Alick Jeffrey made his Rovers debut at the age of 15 years, 229 days in 1954 against Fulham at Belle Vue to become the club's youngest ever player.

Record League Goalscorer

Tom Keetley amassed 180 league goals between 1923 and 1929 for the Rovers following the First World War, with the club being re-elected into the Football League at the start of the decade. Despite his outstanding personal record, the club never managed a finish higher than fourth place and did not achieve promotion during his time with the club.

Highest League Finish

The Rovers' best overall finish came at the end of the 1901/02 season when they finished in seventh place in Division Two during the club's first ever year in the Football League.

Highest Number of points

The club's highest points tally was recorded in 2004 when Rovers finished champions of the Third Division and amassed 92 points from over the course of the league campaign.

Record Transfer Fee Paid

During the summer of 2010 Rovers smashed their transfer record to sign striker Billy Sharp from Sheffield United. Sharp had spent much of the previous season on loan and ended the campaign as the side's top goalscorer which prompted the club to pay a record £1.15 million fee to secure his services on a full-time basis.

Record Transfer Fee Received

During the close season in 2009, Reading paid £2 million to sign Rovers player Matt Mills. The powerful central defender had joined on a full-time basis the year before, having spent a year on loan from Manchester City. The club had paid a then record £300,000 to sign Mills from City so his departure 12 months later represented good business (off the field at least . . .).

THE BEGINNINGS

On a midsummer's evening in 1879, a group of Doncaster's young men met with the intention of forming a football club to represent their town. This was to prove the spark which would lead to one such young man, 18-year-old Albert Jenkins, assembling a group to play in an exhibition game of Association Football against the Yorkshire Institute for the Deaf, following an invitation from the headmaster of the school. Mr Jenkins and his team fought out a 4–4 draw from being 4–0 down and as they walked back into the town a decision was made by those present that they should form a football club under the name 'Doncaster Rovers'.

The first game played as the newly formed club took place on 3 October 1879 at Rawmarsh and also ended in a draw. Doncaster Rovers Football Club had been born. The team would play a number of friendly exhibition matches against local teams throughout the following decade, faring well in terms of results.

In 1872 the club held its first AGM and elected a chairman, secretary, treasurer and committee members and continued to be run with a proficient style. The formation of the Football League in 1888 was, however, still a league too far from the amateur outfit but the side did enter the FA Challenge Cup that season for the first time, with defeat to Rotherham Town in the first qualifying round doing nothing to dampen the rise of the football club.

In 1891, following a season playing in the newly formed Midland Alliance League, the club successfully applied for membership of the Midland League and was crowned champions of that league only 6 years later.

The 1901/02 season saw Rovers make their debut in the Football League following the news that New Brighton had folded, and Doncaster were the club next in line to join, with the club's first ever Football League game being played on 7 September 1901, a creditable and exciting 3–3 draw with Port Vale, and went on to finish in an impressive seventh place in Division Two – which still remains the club's highest ever placing within the Football League.

The side could not reproduce these efforts the following season and finished third from bottom and subsequently, somewhat controversially, failed to be re-elected. Another season in the Midland League ended with re-election back to the Football League with the club taking the step of forming as a limited company, and Doncaster Rovers Football and Athletic Club Ltd was incorporated on 1 July 1904.

On the pitch, however, things didn't go so well and Rovers finished bottom of Division Two, managing only eight points all season – a record which still stands as the fewest points in Football League history! The club failed to achieve re-election following such a dismal display and returned to the Midland League, which would become home for the club for almost 20 years.

Following the First World War the club established itself as one of the best in the Midland League and eventually were voted back where they belonged at the beginning of the 1923/24 season as one of twenty-two clubs in the Football League Division Three (North) – league status the club would retain, unbroken, for some 75 years.

CULT HEROES – MICKEY NORBURY

Mickey Norbury will always be considered something of a hero by Doncaster fans after scoring a hat-trick against Scunthorpe United at Glanford Park in Rovers' 5–0 demolition of their rivals. Former jail bird 'Mental' Mickey joined Rovers in 1994 having enjoyed a good record at Preston North End; however he suffered a broken leg at Deepdale which kept him out for 18 months and his promising career never really recovered. At Rovers he proved a decent, hardworking strike partner for the more skilful Graeme Jones, though he himself didn't find the net throughout the whole of the 1994/95 league season before suddenly scoring 5 goals in as many games. He left the club for Halifax the following season and drifted into the non-league game where he enjoyed some success as a striker in the Conference.

In January 2007, while Goole's assistant manager, he was handed a 6-year touchline ban having been charged with two accounts of foul and abusive language and threatening behaviour towards referees.

'I've had my share of sendings off but never once have I threatened a referee – until this season.' However, happily this ban was later reduced to 182 days following an appeal.

Sometimes hot-headed and occasionally reckless, Mickey was no stranger to red and yellow cards throughout his career, but his performance at Glanford Park made him a cult figure among Rovers fans. In total he made 27 appearances for the Rovers, scoring 5 times.

BEND IT LIKE BECKHAM

David Beckham scored his first Football League goal against Doncaster Rovers while on loan at Preston North End in February 1995. Coming on as a substitute, 19-year-old Beckham scored direct from a corner to help Preston hold the Rovers to a 2–2 draw at Deepdale during a Division Three encounter.

ROVERS GREATS – 1920s

Tom Keetley

One of twelve brothers, four of whom played for the club during the 1920s, Tom Keetley joined the Rovers from Bradford Park Avenue in 1923. He went on to become one of the most significant members of the team. He spent six seasons at Belle Vue and scored more than 20 goals every term, and is Rovers' all-time leading goalscorer with an incredible 180 goals.

During the 1926/27 season, Keetley bagged an amazing 36 league goals in 36 games, an incredible scoring record over the course of a season that never looked like being surpassed. That was, however, until two years later when in 1929 Keetley finished top of the scoring charts with 40 league goals in just 32 matches, including an outstanding performance in a match at Ashington when he scored 6 of the Rovers goals in a 7–4 victory.

He was a legend while at Rovers, so it is understandable that consternation resounded around Belle Vue in October 1928 when he was placed on the transfer list at his own request, having had a disagreement with the board over the terms of his benefit. Eventually the dispute was resolved with the club guaranteeing a sum from a match to be played against Hearts. Evidently, however, the problems with the board were never totally resolved and the following summer Keetley declined to re-sign for the club, instead preferring to move back to Derbyshire to be closer to his business interests there. The fee the club received from Second Division Notts County went towards offsetting the loss the club had accrued the following season, however the loss of Keetley's goals would have left a bigger void in any team than the one on the balance sheet.

The goals continued to flow at his new club, where he still holds the club record for goals scored in a single season with 39, and he scored a total of 94 goals in 103 games for Notts County. When his career ended in 1934 following a brief spell with Lincoln City, he had made a total of 330 league appearances, which yielded a return of 284 goals.

Keetley was a goalscorer the likes of which are seldom seen; his record in a Rovers shirt (185 goals in 241 appearances in all competitions for the club) is unparalleled, with the biggest surprise of all being that Rovers never achieved promotion during his time at the club, despite his goals. Quite simply, Tom Keetley was the club's greatest ever goalscorer.

FEED THE WORLD

During the club's time in non-league football, a number of fans made the trip to Hayes for a Conference match. The game had got underway when the local police decided they had better play things safe and decided to segregate the crowd. A quick shuffle on the terraces had the desired effect, but unfortunately left most of the Rovers fans cut off from the ground's snack bar, leading to the visiting fans spontaneous performance of 'Feed the world, Donny know its dinner time.' However, the song was rather less successful than the Bob Geldof-inspired original, and the journey back to South Yorkshire remained a hungry one.

HOME DRAW ... OR NOT

During the 1934/35 season Doncaster Rovers enjoyed the unusual distinction of not drawing a single home game. The side won 16 out of 21 games on home soil that year and only drew 5 games on their travels en route to winning the Third Division North title, using a total of only 19 players during the 42 matches.

AWAY DAYS

The immediate post-war seasons saw Rovers enjoy some notable successes, winning the Third Division twice. However, both were seasons when Rovers fans would have been best served by watching the team on the road. Unusually, in 1946/47 the team accrued 37 points away from home, winning 19 of 21 matches, as opposed to the 35 points they picked up at home. Amazingly, this anomaly cropped up again in 1949/50 as the team again won the league by picking up 28 points on their travels against 27 at home.

ROVERS GREATS – 1930s

Fred Emery
Following brief spells with Lincoln City and Bradford City, Fred joined Rovers in the summer of 1924 but had to wait until December to make his debut in a 1–0 win at home to Hartlepool when he was drafted in as replacement to the injured full-back Wigglesworth. He made a total of just 11 appearances that season but did play in 4 of the final 5 games. Beginning the following season firmly in the first team, he missed just 4 games all year.

A talented and composed player he was primarily used as a left-half but he had enough quality to play anywhere in defence. Always a reliable and consistent performer he became a key element in the Rovers team, eventually being made club captain for the start of the 1932/33 season.

It was under his guidance as team captain that Rovers won the Third Division North championship during the 1934/35 season; again a picture of consistency he played in all of the club's first 37 league games providing a key component in the Rovers defence.

It was as a result of this experience as skipper, allied with the high regard with which he was held at Belle Vue that led to his appointment as player-manager in 1936, filling the vacancy left by David Menzies' departure. He combined playing with the role of manager for a short time, with his final appearance in a Rovers shirt coming away at Tottenham in April 1936. The following season the team felt his absence on the pitch hard as they conceded 84 league goals and were relegated back to Division Three.

Emery subsequently enjoyed some success over the next two seasons as manager, guiding the club to runners-up spot in Division Three twice, just narrowly missing out on returning the team to the Second Division before the outbreak of the Second World War. During the war-enforced break in the league structure, Emery ended his association with the club in 1940. He went on to manage Carlisle United for a 7-year spell between 1951 and 1958, having replaced future Liverpool manager Bill Shankly, before his death a year later in 1959.

A fixture in the Rovers side for over a decade, he holds the record for the highest number of appearances by a Rovers player, making a total of 437 appearances and scoring 31 goals.

FLOWERS ON THE LINE

On 14 March 1936 Rovers player George Flowers was left out of the side to play Bradford City at Valley Parade in a Division Two game. However, having settled down to watch the match, George's afternoon was to be disturbed when the referee for the fixture failed to turn up. The senior linesman grabbed the whistle and Flowers was pressed into action as the linesman for the afternoon! Despite having 'one of their own' running the line, Rovers lost the game 3–1, with some consolation coming for the league's most hastily inserted linesman after the game, when Flowers received the official's fee of £1 11s 6d.

TOP CUP RUNS

FA Cup 1973/74

The first two rounds of the 1973/74 FA Cup were well won courtesy of a couple of good wins at home. However, the third round was an altogether different prospect. Going into the tie with Liverpool, Rovers were bottom of Division Four, having managed just 5 league wins all season. They travelled to Anfield to meet a Liverpool team sitting second in English football's top tier and who were reigning league champions and UEFA Cup holders. Not surprisingly given no chance, Doncaster remarkably came from behind twice, before coming agonisingly close to snatching a winner in the last minute, with Peter Kitchen's last-gasp effort striking the crossbar. Liverpool were to have too much for the Rovers, winning the replay in fine style 2–0 and then heading to the final, where a Kevin Keegan-inspired performance led the Merseyside giants to their second ever FA Cup win as Bill

Shankly's side ripped Newcastle apart at Wembley. Below is
a summary of Doncaster's FA Cup run:

First Round, 24 November 1973
Doncaster Rovers 1–0 Lincoln City
Murray (Pen)
Rovers: Book, Ternent, Brookes, Irvine, Uzelac, Wignall,
Murray, Woods, Kitchen, Elwiss, O'Callaghan.
Attendance 3,628

Second Round, 15 December 1973
Doncaster Rovers 3–0 Tranmere Rovers
Kitchen
Elwiss
Woods
Rovers: Book, Ternent, Brookes, Irvine, Uzelac, Wignall,
Murray, Woods, Kitchen, Elwiss, O'Callaghan. Sub; Curran
for Ternent.
Attendance 2,444

Third Round, 5 January 1974
Liverpool 2–2 Doncaster Rovers
O'Callaghan
Kitchen
Rovers: Book, Ternent, Brookes, Irvine, Wignall, Uzelac,
Murray, Woods, O'Callaghan, Elwiss, Kitchen.
Attendance 31,483

Third Round replay, 8 January 1974
Doncaster Rovers 0–2 Liverpool
Rovers: Book, Ternent, Brookes, Irvine, Uzelac, Wignall,
Curran, Murray, O'Callaghan, Elwiss, Kitchen.
Attendance 22,499

LOCAL LIEVESLEY

The 1929/30 season opened with Rovers handing a debut to local boy Leslie Lievesley. The 18-year-old Rossington lad made his debut for the club as centre-forward. However, it was to be short-lived as after just 5 minutes of a game played in torrential rain making the pitch difficult to negotiate, Leivesley was forced off with an injury to his leg that meant he would not feature for the side again for 5 months.

When he did reappear, Rovers got a look at what they had been missing as the young forward scored 12 goals in his next 13 games. Les left the club after another successful season the following year, later becoming coach of AC Torino. Sadly he was killed in the Superga air disaster of 1949 that killed many of the Torino team.

GREATEST GAMES

Rovers 6–3 Darlington, 29 September 1964
The 1964/65 season always looked as though it would be difficult, as manager Bill Leivers made wholesale changes to the playing staff during the summer with only 9 players being retained on the club's books. The most notable presence was that of Alick Jeffrey who had returned to the club mid-way through the previous season following a career-threatening injury.

Rovers had begun the season with a mixed bag of results having won half of the first 10 games. In their next game, against Darlington, Rovers had the better of the first half, and with 35 minutes approaching surged forward with some neat passing setting Broadbent free and in space out wide. He had time to look up and deliver a superb pinpoint cross into the box which was met brilliantly by Alick Jeffrey who had timed his run across his marker perfectly to direct a glancing header beyond the despairing dive of O'Neill in the Darlington goal.

Finally the visitors' rearguard had been breached and the home fans sat back in expectation of more of the same but Darlington battled back and within 4 they minutes stunned the home side by drawing level. Yeoman drove the ball deep into the penalty box and with Darlington forward Allison challenging fiercely, the ball dropped to Lawton who fizzed the loose ball home giving Rovers' keeper Oxford no chance. A fantastic half drew to a close at 1–1 with the Rovers players left scratching their heads at how they were not already out of sight. Few could have expected the sensational second-half showing from both sides which totally eclipsed the breathless first 45 minutes.

With the half barely 2 minutes old, Wylie found some space from deep and clipped the ball forward towards the impressive Broadbent who held off the attentions of the Darlington defenders before coolly lobbing the ball over the keeper's head with a finish of real quality which caught everyone by surprise. Belle Vue erupted as the home side put on a superb display of football as Robinson exploded down the right wing before cutting in and darting for the byline before pulling the ball back to Jeffrey, who was in the right place yet again, to hammer home number 3 after 55 minutes.

Within a minute Darlington hit back once more as the game pulsated from end to end. The Rovers defence, seemingly still celebrating the third goal, were caught by a long ball over the top and Allison raced clear before lobbing the ball over the advancing Oxford in a near carbon copy of Broadbent's goal. Suddenly Darlington had dragged themselves back into the match at 3–2.

Still there was no time to catch your breath as from the restart Grainger surged forward for the Rovers, breaking down the left flank before scything the ball into the middle where who else but Alick Jeffrey was once again on hand to prod the ball home, completing a splendid hat-trick and ending a scintillating spell of 3 goals in 3 minutes.

The game then streamed back and forth with both sides still very much in the game and creating chances almost at will before on 75 minutes a fifth Rovers goal put some daylight between the two sides. Grainger again cut straight through the middle of the park, heading for goal when the ball dropped to Broadbent within shooting distance. Without pausing for thought he immediately let fly, only to see his shot blocked and the ball ricochet back to the feet of Grainger who rolled the ball home from close range.

Still the sides exchanged blows, continuing at lightning pace before Rovers added a sixth goal 4 minutes from time. A bad mistake from the Darlington defenders let in Alick Jeffrey, who strolled clear of the last man and almost broke the net to cap a wonderful individual performance and notch his fourth of the afternoon.

To their credit, the visitors refused to lie down and would have certainly still been in the game had it not been for a brilliant display from Rovers keeper Ken Oxford, but even he was helpless with two minutes to go as Darlington deservedly added some credibility to the scoreline. The home side failed to clear the danger on a number of occasions before Lawton spun on a loose ball to snatch a fine goal and complete the scoring at 6–3.

It had certainly been a night to remember as both sides had played some terrific, high-tempo football throughout 90 breathtaking minutes which were a credit to the division. The fantastic gate of 14,103 boosted the home average to 10,394 for the season and earned the players £7 in 'gate' bonuses, but it further served as a great example of the potential surrounding the football club with the result and the manner of the victory providing a glimpse of the abilities of the players and a sign of how things could develop on the playing field.

THEY SAID IT

'The players were magnificent because they were up against some top quality players. We showed people that we can play football and we didn't just lump it.'

Doncaster manager Dave Penney speaks to BBC Sport following the outstanding Carling Cup game against Arsenal

'I didn't have much left in my legs in extra time. I missed a great chance to make it three but Barnesy put it on a plate for me to score the winner. It is the best day of my career.

Fran Tierney on the Conference play-off final at Stoke

'We realise Donny have been playing well. But equally they know how well we've been doing. They're only 19 miles or so up the road and that is going to give the game a lot of spice.'

Sheffield United manager Kevin Blackwell in premature bullish mood. Rovers turned over the Blades at Bramall Lane thanks to a James O'Connor's goal as Rovers won 1–0

RECORD VERSUS RIVALS

Historically Rovers have enjoyed rivalries with each of their South Yorkshire rivals in addition to near neighbours Scunthorpe United from Lincolnshire.

During the club's time in the Football Conference, rivalries emerged with teams such as Rushden & Diamonds (most notably during an ill-tempered FA Cup second round replay), Boston United and Yeovil (during this time the Glovers always seemed to beat Rovers, a streak which followed both teams into the Football League!). However, it is the aforementioned rivalries which burn brightest and here are the details of games between the clubs so far (up to and including the 2010/11 season). . . .

Rovers v Rotherham United

The Millers have clearly had the best of the results between the two clubs and incredibly Rovers have never won a cup tie against Rotherham in 10 attempts. Rovers' best win came in Division Three North with a 4–1 win at Belle Vue on 25 October 1924 thanks to a brace of goals from record goalscorer Tom Keetley, with further strikes from Bailey and Boardman.

	Rovers	Rotherham	Draw
League	23	32	19
FA Cup	0	5	1
League Cup	0	3	1
Total	23	40	21

Rovers v Scunthorpe

Rovers have recorded 5–0 wins against the Iron on two separate occasions. In February 1980 a brace apiece from Alan Warboys and Dave Bentley, along with a goal from Stuart Mell, gave Rovers a comfortable win at Belle Vue in the old Division Four. Rovers produced another 5-star display 15 years later, this time at Glanford Park. Lee Warren and Steve Harper added goals to striker Mickey Norbury's memorable hat-trick to hand Rovers an emphatic win.

	Rovers	Scunthorpe	Draw
League	19	14	19
FA Cup	0	1	0
League Cup	1	1	1
Total	20	16	20

Rovers v Barnsley

Rovers' best win against Barnsley came in a Division Four game in October 1965 with a Ricketts goal, combined with a brace each for the prolific Alick Jeffrey/Laurie Sheffield strike partnership, helping Rovers to a fine 5–1 win at Oakwell. This match took place in front of 13,358 people on Doncaster's way to winning the Division Four championship.

	Rovers	Barnsley	Draw
League	22	22	18
League Cup	1	0	1
Other	1	0	0
Total	24	22	19

Rovers v Sheffield United

Arguably Rovers' most notable win against the Blades came in January 2009 with James O'Connor's scruffy strike sealing a 1–0 win at Bramall Lane on the club's return to the second tier of the English game. The result made up a superb away win on a run of results which transformed Doncaster's fortunes during the season and cemented their place in the Championship.

	Rovers	Sheffield United	Draw
League	5	8	9
FA Cup	0	2	0
League Cup	1	0	1
Total	6	10	10

Rovers v Sheffield Wednesday
Rovers completed a league 'double' over Wednesday during the 2009/10 season; a 1–0 win at the Keepmoat, followed by a 2–0 reverse at Hillsborough, which contributed to the Owls suffering relegation from the Championship.

	Rovers	Sheffield Wed	Draw
League	3	7	2
League Cup	1	4	0
Total	4	11	2

ROVERS GREATS – 1940s

Syd Bycroft
Syd Bycroft joined Doncaster Rovers in January 1936 having made a name for himself playing in the Midland League with Grantham Town. His debut was not long in coming, lining up as a centre-forward in the Rovers first team for a Second Division match at Swansea. Rovers were beaten comfortably 2–0 and Bycroft spent the next few weeks in the Rovers reserves where he was 'reinvented' as a centre-half, making so much progress that he was brought back into the team in March and played in all the club's final 7 games at the heart of the defence and remained a regular from then on.

Syd's career was interrupted by the start of the Second World War when he was assigned the role of police officer following the suspension of the Football League schedule. However, he continued to play regularly for the club during the war and when the league resumed in 1946 he was once again an integral part of the team.

He missed just 1 match during the club's record-breaking season in winning the Third Division championship in 1946/47 and over the subsequent years he became the foundation of the Rovers teams, and they once again won the Third Division title in 1950 with Bycroft ever-present throughout the whole season.

He retired from playing at the end of the 1951/52 season but, having qualified as a coach a few years previously, he stayed on with the club assisting with the coaching and training sessions. In January 1958, following the shock departure of Peter Doherty, Bycroft and trainer Jack Hodgson were placed in joint charge of team affairs until the end of the season. The pair's first game in charge was, by chance, against Peter Doherty's new team, Bristol City. Rovers won 2–1. The season had not been going well for Rovers who were struggling in Division Two and despite winning their opening game, Bycroft and Hodgson could only guide the team to one further win all season with the club subsequently relegated. Bycroft and Hodgson went back to their former duties and a new manager was installed, with Bycroft finally leaving the club in 1959 after a 23-year association.

He made 333 league appearances for the club, scoring twice, but the reality is that had it not been for the war, he would surely have become the club's record league appearance holder (he made in excess of 150 further appearances for the club in the wartime competitions). He had a reputation for being one of the toughest centre-halves in the game; he was fierce in the tackle and was a hard, uncompromising man on the field, but a gentleman off it. He will be forever one of the club's greats.

Clarrie Jordan

Clarrie signed on as a Rovers player just a few weeks before the start of the Second World War began in 1939, meaning he was forced to wait until the Football League resumed its schedule in 1946 before he recorded his League debut. However, the war years saw the club placed in the East Midlands League which provided 20 competitive matches as well as organising a number of 'friendly' matches. These saw a number of guest players used as well as younger players brought in from the reserve side, including a 17-year-old centre-forward called Clarrie Jordan. Jordan in turn made a number of guest appearances for other sides such as Leeds United and Derby County, but turned down their advances with offers of a full-time deal after the war in order to return to the Rovers.

By 1942 Clarrie was regularly included in the Rovers team, scoring over 20 goals in the two seasons prior to the end of the war as the club's leading marksman in each. Jordan finally lined up to make his Football League debut in 1946 in the home win over Rochdale, scoring his first goal in the following game as Rovers beat Chester 3–1. He was instrumental in the club's record-breaking season that year as the team won the Third Division comfortably. Jordan scored 42 league goals in 41 appearances in a remarkable season that saw him notch 4 hat-tricks, with him scoring a total of 44 goals in all competitions.

Clarrie left the club the following season, signing for Sheffield Wednesday, much to the disappointment of the Belle Vue faithful to whom he was a hero, with Rovers receiving a reported £6,000 fee in addition to forward Arnold Lowes. Rovers struggled with life in a higher division and with goals proving difficult to come by, particularly following Jordan's exit, they were subsequently relegated.

Jordan, who remarkably had still been working at South Kirkby Colliery throughout his time at the Rovers, turned full-time as a professional footballer with Wednesday for whom he scored 32 goals in 92 appearances. In total he made 60 league appearances for the Rovers during which he scored 48 goals. However, in reality he scored more than double this for the club if his goals during the war years were included. His 42 league goals in one season remain a club record, as he remains a legend in the history of the football club.

WELCOMING THE AUSTRIANS

In December 1935 the club enjoyed their first experience of a team from foreign shores as they entertained one of Europe's premier sides of the day in FC Austria Vienna in an exhibition game. 3,700 people turned up on a wintry Monday afternoon to see the Austrians' neat, accurate passing game. The visitors took the lead after just 5 minutes before a hand ball on the line let in Albert Turner to equalise from the penalty spot. Turner had the chance to put Rovers ahead, again from the spot, only to hit a post and Molzer, the Austrians' outside right, went on to claim the winner for the visitors late on.

MANAGER HISTORY

Arthur Porter	1920–1
Harry Tufnell	1921–2
Arthur Porter	1922–3
Dick Ray	1923–7
David Menzies	1928–36
Fred Emery	1936–40
Bill Marsden	1944–6
Jackie Bestall	1946–9
Peter Doherty	1949–58
Jack Crayston	1958–9
Jackie Bestall	1959–60
Norman Curtis	1960–1
Danny Malloy	1961–2
Oscar Hold	1962–4
Bill Leivers	1964–6
Keith Kettleborough	1966–7
George Raynor	1967–8
Lawrie McMenemy	1968–71
Morris Setters	1971–4
Stan Anderson	1975–8
Billy Bremner	1978–85
Dave Cusack	1985–7
Dave Mackay	1987–9
Billy Bremner	1989–91
Steve Beaglehole	1991–3
Ian Atkins	1994
Sammy Chung	1994–6
Kerry Dixon	1996–7
Dave Cowling	1997
Mark Weaver	1997–8
Ian Snodin	1998–9
Steve Wignall	1999–2001
Dave Penney	2001–6
Sean O'Driscoll	2006–

THE GROUNDS

Intake Ground, 1885–1916

The Intake Ground played host to the club during its infancy and during its first few steps. It had absolutely no facilities and the teams were forced to get changed and discuss tactics some 500 yards away at a local pub, before making their way down to the ground for the game. Three years into their stay at Intake, the club erected a stand at the side of the playing surface which included turnstiles and a ticket office, with a 'shed' used as a press office added a couple of years later. Unfortunately, the stand was blown down twice in the coming years by particularly inclement Doncaster weather and had to be rebuilt with dressing rooms included around the turn of the century.

The club's record attendance for a match at the Intake Ground was over 6,000 against Middlesbrough in 1902. During the First World War, with the club ceasing operations, the ground was requisitioned by the War Department and used as a military depot.

The Bennetthorpe Ground, 1920–22

After the reformation of the club following the end of the First World War, Rovers were based at the Bennetthorpe Ground as a short-term venue while negotiations were conducted by the council. The club had wanted to move to the Low Pastures site, but restrictions imposed by the local council made an agreement difficult. However, these issues were resolved and the club had a 2-year spell at their temporary home with the team being watched by the club's highest gate on the opening day of the 1921/22 season, with 7,219 people watching the game against Gainsborough Trinity.

Belle Vue, 1922–2006

With negotiations for the Low Pastures site concluded, the club took up the lease and moved into 'Belle Vue' which would become home for more than 80 years. The ground was opened on Saturday 26 August 1922 for the Midland League game against Gainsborough which attracted a crowd of over 10,000.

Belle Vue originally sported a main stand for seating 4,000 spectators with a terraced area in front which catered for a further 3,000. In 1924 shelter was added to the opposite side of the pitch, meaning those standing on the 'Popular side' had the luxury of staying dry! Subsequently, the Main Stand which had been erected at the Bennetthorpe Ground was transported to the new site and dropped into place on the 'Town End' at Belle Vue! By 1935, turnstiles, fencing and gates had been added as the club sought entry into the Football League and the ground had an impressive capacity of around 40,000.

The following years saw a lot of changes to the club, but Belle Vue remained basically the same until 1985 when the Safety of Sports Grounds Act which resulted from the Bradford fire caused major changes. The Town End had to be pulled down and £100,000 worth of fireproofing work carried out to the Main Stand, slashing capacity to around 10,000 before the Hillsborough disaster imposed further restrictions. This in turn reduced capacity to 7,294, though the ground had the unusual distinction of being the only stadium to have separate tunnels for the home and away teams.

Following the club's promotion to the Football League, 'hospitality areas' were introduced to the Town End, with double-storey Portakabins lining the back of the stands until the final game against Nottingham Forest, on Boxing Day 2006.

By the end, Belle Vue was tired, outdated and impractical – but it was home. The crowd was almost on top of the pitch and the atmosphere of a full house inside Belle Vue was unlike any other. I remember clambering over the pot-holed car park, up the old, creaking wooden staircase at the back of the Main Stand. Here I would take my numbingly firm seat on a length of railway sleeper, sitting next to my Dad, watching the game as best as I could through the restricted view afforded by the steel supports in front of the Main Stand. It was, and always will be special, and for me and thousands of others, the name Belle Vue could not have been more apt.

The Keepmoat Stadium, 2007–
The first game came on New Year's Day 2007 as the side beat Huddersfield in a League One match. The record attendance to date at the Keepmoat was 15,002 for a league game against Leeds United in 2008.

The stadium was built at a cost of around £30 million, designed to provide a high-quality sporting environment with a community focus. It has a capacity of 15,231 with improved seating and disabled access bars, club shop, hospitality areas and a mini-stadium on the same site with a 500-seat stand, running track, multiple outdoor training pitches, and a fitness and health centre.

The Keepmoat Stadium has finally dragged the club up to date, with the impressive facilities behind the ground providing a base for Doncaster Rover's continued success. In time the Keepmoat will produce its own stars, its own names and, most importantly, its own memories.

THEY SAID IT

'It doesn't get anywhere near when we got back in the Football League but it is up there.'

Dave Penney refusing to get carried away following the outstanding cup win over Villa

'We are playing champagne football, as good as anyone in Yorkshire!'

John Ryan, always happy to get carried away

'I knew they would not run out of steam. They are a good footballing side. There was not much in it in the first half, but they were better than us in the second half. We did want to do well in the competition, but the penalty decision knocked the stuffing out of us a bit and the second goal killed us.'

Villa manager David O'Leary after Doncaster's cup win

GREATEST GAMES

Rovers 1–0 Leeds United 25 May 2008, play-off final
The 2007/08 season had trundled along in truly inauspicious fashion before Rovers burst into life over the Christmas period, only to miss out on automatic promotion on the last day of the season. The disappointment was put to one side with the 5–1 play-off semi-final demolition of Southend and all eyes were on the final, against Leeds United. The approach to Wembley, covered in red and white hoops, was an image which will live long in the memory.

Rovers flew out of the traps and, with only 6 minutes gone, Jason Price's right-footed shot was deflected inches over the bar. The game was explosive, played at a tempo dictated by the Rovers midfield, and Wellens fired into the side-netting before Coppinger was denied by keeper Ankergren's dive at his feet, when he looked certain to score.

Striker James Hayter also went close with a splendid turn and shot which just cleared the crossbar. Rovers continued to push forward, with Leeds' only effort of note coming two minutes before the interval – Jonathon Howson's shot curling over Neil Sullivan's goal.

The game was still finely poised as Rovers got the second half underway, attacking towards the hordes of Rovers fans. Driving forward once again, Captain Brian Stock took a 47th-minute corner, swinging the ball in from the right. Price looked to be the obvious choice and made a near-post run, taking two defenders with him, but the flight of the ball beat them all and arrowed into the middle of the box where James Hayter, alone on the penalty spot, produced a superb diving header to power the ball past the helpless Ankergren from 12 yards out. The sight of the ball bouncing up into the net was greeted by deafening wall of sound from the Rovers end of a packed Wembley Stadium which erupted in sheer delight as the club's then record signing wheeled away in front of a sea of red and white to be mobbed by team-mates, having finally handed his team a much-deserved lead.

The next twenty minutes flew by in a blur as the contest evened out, with Leeds looking to find a way back into the game. However, it was Rovers who almost extended their lead, James Coppinger running clear on the right, only to be denied by a superb last-ditch challenge. Into the last 10 minutes and Leeds had to press forward but could not find any way through a resolute Rovers defence and as the clock ticked agonizingly into the 96th minute the referee glanced at his watch and finally relented, sparking incredible scenes of celebration. It was a result and an occasion which had been 129 years in the making as thousands of dreams made in South Yorkshire came gloriously true under Wembley's arch.

Rovers had been immense to a man, winning the game but having played the type of good quality, passing football, which the team was fast becoming known for, throughout 90-odd pulsating and nail-biting minutes.

Brian Stock led the victorious side up the famous steps and became the first Rovers captain ever to lift a trophy at Wembley, and in doing so etched an indelible image on an unforgettable day which was probably the finest in the history of the club.

CULT HEROES – FRAN TIERNEY

Fran Tierney was one of the highly regarded players to come off the Crewe Alexandra production line, during a period when Dario Gradi produced a number of top-class talents such as Danny Murphy, Robbie Savage and Neil Lennon. Tierney was regarded as the hottest of prospects in the early part of his career and was reportedly set for a high-profile move to Liverpool in the mid-1990s before a serious knee injury scuppered the deal.

He signed for Rovers in March 2001 having had brief spells with Notts County and Exeter City. There were still question marks over his fitness, though, having never really moved on from injury. Fran's time at the Rovers, as throughout his career, was littered with injuries. However, when fit he proved he had the ability to play at a much higher level. Skilful on the ball he had great vision and awareness and could provide a quality final ball with either foot. He is indelibly etched on the history of the club, as it was his goal in extra time which won the Conference play-off final in 2003 and lifted the club back into the Football League. Sadly, injury eventually had the final say and ended the midfielder's career in late 2004.

DISASTERS ...

In August 1993 Rovers travelled to Blackpool for the second leg of a League Cup first round tie. 1–0 down from the first leg, not much was expected from the Rovers team. However, all of that dramatically changed inside half an hour as goals from Kevin Hulme, Steve Harper and Russ Wilcox gave Rovers a seemingly unassailable 3–0 lead, leading the tie 3–1 on aggregate. I was there that night and it was a bitterly cold evening on the west coast but even when Watson pulled one back for Blackpool it did little to dampen the mood as Rovers were cruising. It was my own fault really as I had seen enough of Rovers to never be complacent and sure enough, Quinn and big Dave Bamber added to the scoring and Rovers threw away a 3-goal lead which not only meant a 3–3 draw on the night, but that the Rovers crashed out of the cup 4–3 on aggregate. A night when, after 30 minutes it looked harder to get beaten than see the game out, Rovers somehow managed a disaster!

MANAGERIAL GREATS – DAVE PENNEY

Dave Penney joined the club as a player under Ian Snodin during the club's first season in the Conference, becoming a favourite among the Rovers fans. However, by the end of the following season the Rovers found themselves fifth from bottom at the foot of the Conference and in real danger of dropping even further down the non-league pyramid. The Snodins were relieved of their duties at the end of April 2000 and Penney and Mark Atkins were put in temporary control, combining playing with managing the team.

The pair did an excellent job, winning 4 of their 6 games at the helm and guiding the team comfortably clear of relegation. Steve Wignall was installed as the new manager during the summer, but at Christmas 2001 he paid the price for a disappointing start to the season and Dave Penney was named as manager on a full-time basis.

He guided Rovers to a much-improved fourth place in the Conference at the end of the season and made some shrewd additions to key areas of the squad, like defenders Dave Morley and Steve Foster and midfielders Ricky Ravenhill and John Doolan. He also had the ability to get the best out of players such as Paul Barnes, Fran Tierney and Paul Green who were already at the club, and guided the Rovers to a third-place finish and back into the Football League following a memorable win in the play-off final at Stoke.

Immediately installed as favourites for relegation, Penney kept faith with the bulk of the squad which had served him so well in the Conference, again complimented by some astute and eye-catching acquisitions, with experienced target-man Leo Fortune-West providing a different option up front and the capture of highly rated winger Michael McIndoe from Yeovil proving invaluable. Later in the season, Penney again raised eyebrows with his prowess in the transfer market by securing highly rated 18-year-old striker Chris Brown on loan from Sunderland. Brown's partnership with Gregg Blundell provided the catalyst as Rovers defied all expectations and fired themselves to the Third Division title, finishing 4 points ahead of Hull City in the final reckonings, as Dave Penney secured magnificent back-to-back promotions.

The 2004/05 season was another successful campaign, with Rovers more than matching those clubs around them, and they only narrowly missed out on the play-offs as the side's form fell away towards the end of the season.

At the beginning of the 2005/06 season Penney added striker Paul Heffernan and midfielder Sean Thornton to the side, in doing so breaking the club's transfer record twice, with the season expected to see Rovers mount a serious challenge for a third promotion in four seasons. Things started as expected with Rovers around the play-offs – however, it was the Carling Cup that saw Penney extract the most out of his talented squad. Reaching the quarter-finals having beaten Manchester City and thrashing Aston Villa en route, they led Arsenal 2–1 deep into extra time before World Cup winner Gilberto grabbed a cruel equaliser and the Gunners squeezed through on penalties. The performances of his side had attracted huge attention from the national media and Dave Penney was considered to be one of the top up-and-coming English managers. However, the disappointment of the club's heartbreaking exit from the cup took its toll on the side's league campaign as they lost 5 of the next 7 games, a run which ultimately was the team's undoing as Rovers finished 8th, just 2 points outside the coveted play-off places.

More big names joined the club in the summer but the side struggled at the beginning of the season with a poor run which saw only one win in the opening 5 league games, and amid rumours of problems in the dressing room, Rovers parted company with one of the club's most successful ever managers on 28 August 2006.

Dave Penney is regarded as an excellent man-manager who demands a huge amount of passion and respect from his players. His time with the Rovers was characterised by a 4-4-2 formation with the emphasis of pace going forward, two wingers and two strikers, built on a solid defence.

Arguably not the most tactical manager, Penney did have a knack of getting the most from his players and although his teams were set up relatively simply, they always played football the right way and moved the ball about on the floor, with purpose.

He achieved huge success for Doncaster, eventually winning the hard slog to get out of the Conference, strolling to the Third Division title against everyone's expectations and those cold, crowded nights at Belle Vue in the Carling Cup will never be forgotten. For all the club's successes now, it was the achievements and foundations laid by Dave Penney that have ultimately made it possible, and it is a shame that he was probably a victim of his own success, continually over-achieving and exceeding expectations.

Record

	Played	Won	Lost	Drawn
As caretaker	6	4	1	1
As manager	241	114	65	62
Total	247	118	66	63

A FLYING START

In the 1900/01 season Rovers made a flying start to their Midland League campaign winning all of their first 10 matches and scoring a massive 45 goals in the process! Sadly, the side had obviously peaked too soon and went on to lose 7 of the remaining 16 league games and, despite their haul of points from the first half of the season, only managed to stumble into the runners-up spot.

A CROWDED SEASON

Rovers' highest ever average attendance was recorded during the 1950/51 season when they enjoyed a decent season in Division Two, finishing in a very healthy 11th place. The team did so in front of some bumper crowds that season, including gates of over 30,000 for games against Manchester City, Hull City and Luton Town, meaning the average for the year was a record-breaking 22,838.

ROVERS GREATS – 1950s

Alick Jeffrey
Born in Rawmarsh on 29 January 1939, Alick showed early promise and played for Yorkshire and England schoolboys. Just prior to leaving school, the Manchester United manager Matt Busby invited Alick to sign for United only to find the youngster had already agreed to sign for Peter Doherty and Doncaster Rovers. Busby missed out, but promised that Jeffrey would be a United player before long.

Alick made his first appearance in September 1954 in a strong Rovers side (aged just 15), which was tipped to challenge for promotion from Division Two. He scored his first goal for the club in January 1955 in the side's 3–2 win at home to Plymouth, before hitting the headlines with a splendid cup brace against First Division Aston Villa. Jeffrey had become a regular in the first team at 16 and ended the season with an impressive return of 9 goals but there was clearly more to follow. The next season, still in his mid-teens, he notched a further 13 league goals but it was the following year that the youngster would really explode onto the scene. The striker simply blew the opposition away scoring 15 times in just 13 games at the start of the 1956/57 campaign and, at only 18 years of age he was one of the hottest properties in English football. A spell of 6 goals in 3 games prompted Busby to make good his word and United began negotiations to sign the talented forward in October 1956. The deal all but complete, the clubs agreed Jeffrey would sign following the England under-23 international against France that month, only for fate to deliver a cruel blow. During the game Alick sustained a double fracture to his right leg. Complications followed forcing him out of the game, with the FA eventually awarding him compensation for a career-ending injury, and English football had been robbed of one of its finest young talents.

Understandably heartbroken, Alick went to non-league Skegness Town determined to make a recovery, only to receive another setback by breaking his other leg. This would surely have proved too much for most people but Jeffrey fought back for a second time and after months of further hard work he was ready to rejoin Rovers and try to resurrect his career in late 1963, with a season best 11,719 fans turning out to witness his comeback. Alick was soon back among the goals and his partnership with Laurie Sheffield helped the club win the league in 1966 with the pair scoring 50 goals between them. Tragedy, however, was never far away and the following season Alick and club captain John Nicholson were involved in a car accident. Devastatingly, John was killed and Alick was out of action for months.

Understandably things were never quite the same from then on and Alick left the club in 1969. In total he had made 294 appearances for the club, scoring 140 goals; he was president of the club up to his death in December 2000.

Alick is universally accepted as being the club's greatest-ever player. Tremendous with either foot, a strong, powerful runner who was a great finisher, who knows what he may have achieved had he not been injured as an 18-year-old? History was robbed of a player who could have surely gone on to be one of the greatest of a golden generation. Even with his career at Belle Vue so devastatingly curtailed, he is still remembered with great fondness and admiration by all.

TURN ON THE LIGHTS

The first ever floodlit fixture at Belle Vue was a Midland League match between the Rovers reserve side and Lincoln City reserves on 17 February 1953. The game ended 2–2 with 2,170 people turning out to watch the clash.

DOUBLE EIGHT

During the 1946/47 season Rovers were the only club in the entire Football League to enjoy the notable achievement of scoring 8 or more goals on two occasions. The Rovers hammered Carlisle United 9–2 on 25 January 1947 and then thrashed Barrow 8–0 on 13 March 1946 on their way to the Third Division North championship.

TOP CUP RUNS

FA Cup 1954/55
The Rovers best-ever performance in the FA Cup is the fifth round, and while the side managed this four times during the 1950s, the cup run of 1954/55 was undoubtedly the

most notable. A relatively comfortable third round win away at Watford landed Rovers, playing in the second tier at the time, the chance to host Division One side Aston Villa. The tie, played in front of a season's best crowd of over 27,000, was fiercely fought with Rovers giving no ground to their more illustrious opponents and ended in a 0–0 stalemate.

The replay at Villa Park a few days later was just as competitive, with Rovers taking the lead after 18 minutes following a well-worked Tindall goal. Villa struck back, however, and within 10 minutes of the second half went 2–1 up, only for Mooney to equalise, sending the tie into extra time which would still prove not to be decisive.

The following Monday the two sides took to the field again, this time on neutral soil at Maine Road, Manchester. Alick Jeffrey, then only 16 years old, put the Rovers ahead but a second-half equaliser forced the two sides to a third replay at Sheffield Wednesday's Hillsborough. Once again there was nothing between the sides, forcing the clubs to schedule a fourth replay at The Hawthorns. Rovers got off to a great start and led 2–0 inside the hour thanks to Jeffrey and Geoff Walker. Villa pulled one back but Jeffrey was on hand to snatch the winner with 3 minutes to go.

The reward for winning this gruelling series of battles was a trip to Birmingham City in the fifth round four days later, where a visibly jaded Rovers side were beaten 2–1 despite yet another spirited performance.

It was a cup run to be remembered, for the epic series of games between Rovers and Villa, but also for the manner in which the tie was eventually settled. The brace of goals scored by Alick Jeffrey, only two weeks after his 16th birthday, against opponents from the top division of English football, served to further enhance the growing reputation of a rising star within the game.

Third Round, 8 January 1955

Watford   0–2   Doncaster Rovers
Tindall (2)

Rovers: Hardwick, Makepeace, Graham, Gavin, Lawlor, Herbert, Mooney, Tindall, McMorran, Brown, G. Walker.
Attendance: 17,130

Fourth Round, 29 January 1955

Doncaster Rovers   0–0   Aston Villa

Rovers: Hardwick, Makepeace, Graham, Gavin, Williams, Herbert, Mooney, Jeffrey, Tindall, McMorran, G. Walker.
Attendance: 27,767

Fourth Round replay, 2 February 1955

Aston Villa   2–2   Doncaster Rovers
Tindall
Mooney

Rovers: Hardwick, Makepeace, Gavin, Hunt, Williams, Herbert, Mooney, Jeffrey, Tindall, McMorran, G. Walker.
Attendance: 36,522

Fourth Round second replay, 7 February 1955

Doncaster Rovers   1–1   Aston Villa   (at Maine Road)
Jeffrey

Rovers: Hardwick, Makepeace, Graham, Hunt, Williams, Herbert, Mooney, McMorran, J. Walker, Jeffrey, Tindall.
Attendance: 15,047

Fourth Round third replay, 14 February 1955

Doncaster Rovers   0–0   Aston Villa   (at Hillsborough)

Rovers: Hardwick, Makepeace, Graham, Hunt, Williams, Herbert, Mooney, Tindall, J. Walker, Jeffrey, G. Walker.
Attendance: 16,117

Fourth Round fourth replay, 15 February 1955
Doncaster Rovers   3–1   Aston Villa
                              (at The Hawthorns)
Jeffrey (2)
G. Walker
Rovers: Hardwick, Makepeace, Graham, Hunt, Williams, Herbert, Mooney, Tindall, J. Walker, Jeffrey, G. Walker.
Attendance: 18,117

Fifth Round, 19 February 1955
Birmingham City   2–1   Doncaster Rovers
                              Mooney
Rovers: Hardwick, Makepeace, Graham, Hunt, Williams, Herbert, Mooney, J. Walker, Tindall, Nicholson, G. Walker.
Attendance: 57,830

A FAMILY AFFAIR

During the 1920s the Rovers was said to have 'belonged to the Keetleys' with four of the Keetley brothers turning out for the club. Frank, Harold, Joe and most famously Tom Keetley all played for the Rovers in the Third Division during the decade, notching up a combined total of 390 league appearances and scoring a total of 233 league goals.

HAIR TODAY ...

During March 2010 the Rovers were forced to operate under some quite 'hairy' circumstances. The players and staff, led by defender James Chambers, went the entire month of March without shaving in a bid to raise as much money as possible for two fantastic causes. Money raised from this fuzzy exercise was donated to the National Society for the Prevention of Cruelty to Children and the Right to Play charity which helps disadvantaged children in warzones and deprived countries. It was a great initiative which raised just short of £4,000!

MANAGERIAL GREATS – JACKIE BESTALL

At the end of February 1946 Rovers manager Billy Marsden's dispute with the club's directors over the status of his job finally came to a head. Marsden, who combined the manager's duties with being a Sheffield hotel licensee, felt he had successfully combined the two jobs and was confident he could continue to do so into the future. The directors were of a different opinion, however. They were anxious to move the club forward and they felt a full-time manager was the best way to achieve this. There was always only ever going to be one winner in a difference of opinion such as this, and Marsden promptly found himself relieved of his duties and Rovers appointed Jackie Bestall, a veteran of over 400 playing appearances for Grimsby Town, as full-time manager for the 1946/47 season, the first full season following the Second World War.

He made only one signing, Jackie Thompson from Sheffield Wednesday, and was otherwise satisfied with a playing staff which boasted such names as Syd Bycroft, Bert Tindall and Clarrie Jordan. The side made a blistering start to the campaign which the rest of the division simply could not match all season. Winning their first 5 games, the side never looked back, playing an attractive game that yielded plenty of goals. Bestall delivered the Division Three North title, breaking a host of league and club records along the way, dropping only 12 points all season.

Bestall spent the close season on the road, travelling the country looking for new players, only to find that the club simply could not match the going rate and he was forced to start the new season with no new additions. Goals proved harder to come by, a fact worsened by Jordan's departure to Sheffield Wednesday, and with a tight budget not allowing the quality required for a higher level, Rovers slipped to relegation, with Bestall ultimately replaced as manager.

It was a role he would return to, however, a decade later. He was reappointed manager from his role as chief scout in March 1959 with the club in a mess. Successive relegations following the success of the Peter Doherty era saw the club back in the bottom division, average attendances had slipped to about 6,500 – the worst for 30 years – and there had been numerous changes at all levels of the club against the backdrop of financial problems. The club was in decline.

A clearout of the playing staff was required as Bestall looked to rebuild the team, bringing in a number of experienced names who had the attributes necessary to compete at this level. Unsurprisingly the team struggled during the first half of the season and were stuck around the bottom end of the table until the New Year when they once again found their scoring touch which had been a trademark of Bestall's previous regime. Rovers moved up the table, finishing a respectable 17th.

Bestall stood down 2 games into the following season, the club's decline arrested to a point, and a new emphasis placed on once again bringing players through the club's youth system. By 1966 Rovers were beginning to enjoy the dividends of these foundations, built at least in part by Bestall. By February they were sitting in the top six and going well, with a team containing quality players of the likes of Alick Jeffrey, Laurie Sheffield and Tony Coleman.

These achievements looked as though they might be derailed as manager Bill Leivers resigned out of the blue for 'personal reasons'. Once again the board turned to their chief scout and Bestall pushed their drive to promotion on further. Following the tightest of run-ins, Rovers edged out Luton, Torquay and Darlington, finished as champions above the latter on goal difference alone and Bestall was once again celebrating winning the championship. Always intended as a temporary measure, Bestall once again stood down the following December for the board to appoint a long-term successor.

Jackie Bestall will forever be remembered as the manager behind that record-breaking season in the 1940s. Always willing to step in and help the club in times of need, he is the only manager to have won two championships for Rovers, with whom he enjoyed a long and profitable association.

First spell, 1946–9

Played	Won	Lost	Drawn
123	60	37	26

Second spell, 1959–60

Played	Won	Lost	Drawn
63	23	25	15

Third spell, 1966–7

Played	Won	Lost	Drawn
48	20	14	14

Total

Played	Won	Lost	Drawn
234	103	76	55

ROVERS TURN GREEN

Rovers looked decidedly off-colour for the Championship game against Crystal Palace in May 2009. The game saw Rovers wearing a slightly different home kit for the very first time in a one off, to demonstrate the club's support for the National Society for the Prevention of Cruelty to Children. Doncaster wore a special green and white hooped shirt, green shorts and socks with the NSPCC logo replacing the usual sponsor and after the game the shirts worn by the players were auctioned off with all the money raised going directly to the charity.

ROVERS GREATS – 1960s

Laurie Sheffield

Laurie joined Rovers in the summer of 1965 having already established himself as a goalscorer during a 3-year stay at Newport County. There he had broken the post-war goalscoring record, scoring 27 goals during the 1964/65 season and in total scored 46 in 91 appearances for County.

His arrival at Belle Vue saw him team up with Alick Jeffrey in what is still considered one of Rovers' most deadly strike forces. Laurie's impact was immediate – making his debut against Lincoln City at Belle Vue on the opening day of the season, he scored twice as Rovers won 4–0.

Sheffield was outstanding all season and constantly among the goals with he and Jeffrey scoring a massive 50 league goals between them, with Laurie claiming the lion's share of 28 to finish as the club's leading goalscorer. His goals fired the team to the top places in Division Four, and in a close run-in, Rovers clinched the championship and promotion.

The following season started brightly until the tragic car accident that took the life of defender John Nicholson shook the club. The team began to struggle for results but Laurie still continued to find the net regularly and it came as a great surprise to everyone when he joined Norwich in November 1966 for a fee of £12,000. It caused uproar among Rovers fans who were angry at seeing one of the club's most prized possessions depart, especially as he had already scored 14 goals that season in just 21 appearances.

He notched a hat-trick for Norwich on his debut and was a regular name on the score-sheet for them, as he was during spells with Rotherham, Oldham and Luton before returning to Belle Vue in October 1969. Again his impact was immediate, scoring in a 3–1 win at Walsall. Injury disrupted his second spell, however, and he was only able to make 17 starts for the club but still scored 7 goals before ending his career at Peterborough United.

Not the biggest of forwards, he was still excellent in the air and a strong leader of the front line. He was a talented footballer with good vision and awareness of others around him. A genuine goalscorer, he managed 48 goals in 85 games for the club and is still, rightly, considered to be one of the club's finest ever players.

CHAMPIONSHIP-WINNING SEASONS

Division Three North 1934/35

Pld 21	W 16	D 0	L 5	F 53	A 21	Pts 37

Expectations were high before the season started with many people expecting a successful season on the pitch. With only 1 defeat in the club's first 11 games it seemed that optimism was further cemented before consecutive defeats against Chesterfield and Mansfield threatened to see the wheels come off as the club only managed 1 further win until December, prompting the management to dip into the transfer market to acquire the services of forward Reg Baines from Sheffield United.

A remarkable run during January saw the Rovers win 8 games on the bounce and score 29 goals in the process (Baines scored 11 of them, highlighting the impact he had on the team). A couple of defeats around Easter didn't dent the club's hopes too much and they were eventually crowned champions with three games to spare. Nineteen players had played for the club over the course of the season with full-back Shaw present throughout. Winger Albert Turner finished as top scorer with 25 goals, while Baines was not far behind on 21, despite having played 12 fewer games. The club were celebrating promotion to Division Two and their first piece of silverware.

Division Three North 1946/47
Pld 42   W 33   D 6   L 3   F 123   A 38   Pts 72

The first season following the Second World War saw Rovers charge towards the Division Three title right from the first game, winning 11 of the first 12 league matches with goals in plentiful supply.

The side clearly picked up the habit of winning early on and it was a familiar feeling throughout the whole season. There was a spectacular run of 10 wins in a row (including a 9–2 win at home to Carlisle and an 8–0 home victory over Barrow) from January to April 1947 putting them comfortably in the driving seat in the race for the title, which was won well before the team were presented the shield at half time in the final match of the season.

It was an incredible season for the club which saw a number of records broken along the way including the most wins in a season (33), most away wins in a season (18), most consecutive away wins (7), most points in a season (72 – 2 points for a win), and the record for fewest defeats in a season was also equalled (just 3). Maddison and McFarlane were ever-present during the season and Clarrie Jordan topped the scoring charts with a club record 42 goals in 41 league games and 44 goals in all competitions.

Division Three North 1949/50

Pld 42   W 19   D 17   L 6   F 66   A 38   Pts 55

The 1949/50 season was the first with Peter Doherty installed as player-manager of the side, and marked the beginning of arguably the finest era in the club's history with him at the helm. The team enjoyed a bright start, with Doherty contributing the lion's share of the goals, and only lost once in the first 19 games of the season, sitting nicely on top of the table heading into the Christmas period. However, there was little in the way of festive cheer for the Rovers as they failed to win in 4 games, prompting Doherty to spend a record fee on forward Ray Harrison from neighbours Sheffield United. Harrison scored on his debut in a fine 5–1 home win and the Rovers were up and running once more.

Fuelled by Doherty goals the side were soon back on top, and despite a run of only 1 win in the last 7 matches, they always looked too strong for the rest and never gave up top spot. It would have been more comfortable had they won some of the games they drew (17 draws in total) but in the end the championship was won and Rovers headed to Division Two and the club's most successful ever decade.

Division Four 1965/66

Pld 46   W 24   D 11   L 11   F 85   A 54   Pts 59

Goals were never likely to be a problem for the Rovers going into the season, as the previous year's top scorer, Alick Jeffrey, was paired with the newly acquired services of fellow front man Laurie Sheffield. The signs were good right from the off as Rovers won the first 2 games of the season 4–0 with Jeffrey and Sheffield both scoring 3 each.

The pair's partnership flourished and in a team which also contained the likes of Nicholson, Wylie, Ricketts, Gilfillon and Coleman, the Rovers were always going to be there or thereabouts in the final reckonings, and a 7-game unbeaten spell up to the Christmas period put them right in the mix.

Heading into Easter the race was wide open with seven clubs all in touch at the top but Rovers edged ahead in early May thanks to an excellent 2–1 win at home to Barnsley. The next game was lost at home to Notts County (a game which included the infamous Tony Coleman incident) but the side won the next at Crewe before picking up a point at Bradford on the final day to be confirmed as champions.

Sheffield and Jeffrey scored 50 league goals between them during the season, well over half of the team's total, and were rightly the most feared pairing in the division having played a huge part in winning the trophy for their team.

Division Four 1968/69

Pld 46   W 20   D 18   L 8   F 65   A 38   Pts 59

The side started brightly, losing just one of the opening 5 games, before providing a glimpse of what they were capable of by winning the next 5 games in a row to find themselves second in the league standings. Results stuttered slightly through November and George Raynor was replaced by

Lawrie McMenemy as manager. Rovers struggled for goals but were still around the top teams in the division before heading on a superb 20-match unbeaten run, the highlight of which was undoubtedly a 7–0 thrashing of Aldershot at Belle Vue. Top scorer Alick Jeffrey (12 league goals) had left the club at the New Year but the side based their game on a frugal defence and continued to pick up points (of those 20 games unbeaten, 12 were draws) and went on to win 2 of the last 3 games. This included a fine 3–1 at Grimsby on the final day, to be crowned as champions, a couple of points clear at the top.

The side conceded a then club record of only 38 goals during the season and kept 22 clean sheets, which formed the foundation on which the season's success was built.

Division Three 2003/04

Pld 46　　W 27　　D 11　　L 8　　F 79　　A 37　　Pts 92

Rovers went into the season having just regained their Football League status and despite a couple of important close-season additions, were immediately installed as one of the favourites for relegation that year. The team surprised many by winning their opening game 3–1 at Leyton Orient and enjoyed a decent start to the campaign. They were comfortably mid-table following the first 8 games before a 2–0 win at home to Oxford sparked an amazing run of results. It saw the Rovers win an incredible 13 of the next 15 league games, including an excellent 5–1 win at home to Bristol Rovers and a superb 3–1 victory over Swansea, to move to the top of the table on Boxing Day. A couple of defeats saw the side slip to third but an unbeaten February, which yielded 3 wins out of 4, saw them regain top spot and not relinquish it for the remainder of the season.

A series of important draws were followed by some crucial wins, notably at Yeovil and Bristol City. These results ultimately saw Dave Penney's team secure the championship before being crowned champions on the final day of the season following a 1–0 win at home to Carlisle. They finished 4 points clear of nearest rivals Hull City having amassed a club record 92 points.

The nucleus of the side, Warrington, Foster, Green, Blundell and McIndoe, all only missed a handful of games, and along with some important loan signings, provided the consistency required to mount such a strong challenge all season. Notably, four Rovers players reached double figures in the league with Blundell (18), Fortune-West (11), Brown (10) and McIndoe (10) all contributing with important goals.

CULT HEROES – JOHN DOOLAN

Midfielder John Doolan signed for the Rovers at the latter end of the club's stay in the Conference, quickly establishing himself in the centre of Rovers' midfield during Doncaster's rise through the divisions. A talented midfielder who was comfortable on the ball and always able to link play well, Doolan will be forever loved for the part he played during a splendid 3–1 win on a wintry, misty October evening at Oakwell in 2004.

Those who looked hard enough through the Barnsley fog that night, saw John enter into a 'hard' challenge with his opposing number, Stephen McPhail, as the two fought for dominance in the middle of the park. McPhail ended up in a heap on the other side of the advertising hoardings, a result which forever endeared the Scouse midfielder to all Rovers fans, and instantly made him (still to this day) about as welcome in Barnsley as a skunk at a dinner party.

The return game at Belle Vue was drenched in cries of, 'Watch out, Doolan's behind you!' and taunts of 'Doolan's gonna get you!' as Rovers once again hammered Barnsley (4–0) with the big man himself contributing a rare goal, bagging the Rovers' third.

He went on to enjoy successful spells with Blackpool and Rochdale after departing Doncaster in 2005 having made 84 league appearances for the Rovers, scoring twice.

PILOTS BEWARE

The old floodlights at Belle Vue were the only ones in the country to come complete with red aircraft warning lights perched on top to alert passing pilots. This was because the old Doncaster Airport site was situated close to the ground!

ILLUMINATING THE NORTH

In the 1950s the Rovers played their first matches under the newly installed floodlights at Belle Vue. To help pay for them the club played a series of friendly matches under the lights, and on 4 March they made history by becoming the first in the north of England, indeed the first outside London, to play a match under floodlights when Scottish side Hibernian visited Belle Vue with a crowd of over 18,000 turning out to see the visitors win 3–0.

GREATEST GAMES

Rovers 3–2 Dagenham, 10 May 2003

The newspapers claimed it was to be the biggest game in the history of the club, and arguably the Conference play-off final in May 2003 still remains so. Rovers, considered by many to be the biggest club in the Conference, had battled for five years to try to regain their Football League status. They now found the prize only one game away following a season which had seen manager Dave Penney guide the club to a 3rd-place finish and qualify for the first ever play-offs from the Conference.

Having beaten Chester on penalties in the semi-final, thousands of Rovers fans travelled to Stoke's Britannia Stadium to witness the drama. Rovers started the game favourites and included the Conference's golden boot winner in top scorer Paul Barnes up front with key midfielder Paul Green included in midfield. Those two were seen as central figures if the Rovers were to live up to their billing.

Rovers started the first half superbly with Paul Green and Ricky Ravenhill taking control of the midfield, and they went close early on when Fran Tierney's drive was tipped round the post. Midfielder Jamie Paterson also had a shot saved before Paul Barnes was denied by Dagenham keeper Tony Roberts when the Rovers top scorer really should have put his side ahead.

Rovers seemed in control of the proceedings but couldn't find a breakthrough as Steve Foster had a great header scrambled off the line just past the half-hour mark. The Rovers pressure was constant, though, and 6 minutes later they finally got what they deserved; Tim Ryan dug a great ball out from the left and Paul Green, who was outstanding all afternoon, arrived to meet the ball in the box and direct his header home.

Nerves were still present among the Rovers fans during half time as 1 goal is seldom enough – despite Rovers dominance – but the team emerged for the second half in similar mood. Ten minutes after the restart, Tristram Whitman worked the ball to Paterson whose snap shot was diverted for a corner. Central defender Dave Morley nipped in at the near post to head home the resulting cross and Rovers were 2–0 up.

It looked all over at that point, but nerves began to creep into the Rovers side, and Dagenham, now with nothing to lose, began to push forward. Almost out of the blue, Dagenham's much-travelled striker Mark Stein fired home after 63 minutes and then with 15 minutes to go, full-back Tarkan Mustafa made a superb run into the box and finished well past Andy Warrington to stunned silence among the Rovers fans.

The game could now go either way and if no 'golden goal' were forthcoming in extra time, the tie would be settled on penalties. Penney had made a couple of changes to provide fresh legs but extra time was understandably tense, as nerves jangled with neither team wanting to give anything away. With only 10 minutes remaining, Paul Barnes found some room on the left-hand side of the penalty area and clipped the ball across to Tierney who nipped in to roll the ball past Roberts for the most golden of goals and win the tie for the Rovers.

That image of Tierney turning away with his right arm aloft seemed to be frozen in time before a wall a noise greeted the Rovers winger. Suddenly it was all over. The outpouring of relief on the pitch was matched only by the Rovers fans in the stands as the significance of the moment became clear; all the hard work that went before had finally paid off and the Rovers were back where they belonged. The biggest game in the club's history had become one of its finest moments.

TERRIFIC TURF

The pitch at Belle Vue was laid on top of an ash tip, which meant that the turf always drained well. Always immaculate, with the turf kept in tip-top condition, it was rumoured that the Rovers pitch was wanted by Wembley Stadium!

ROVERS GREATS – 1970s

Peter Kitchen

Kitchen came through the youth team before signing a professional contract with Rovers in July 1970 under manager Lawrie McMenemy. The talented striker made progress in reserve team football before being given his chance in a Rovers team that was finding life in the Third Division hard, with goals few and far between. The 18-year-old was included in the starting line-up on 27 November 1970 away at Shrewsbury Town where he made an immediate impact. Within moments the teenager had opened the scoring, and went on to have a hand in Rovers' third as the side recorded a great 3–0 win. He kept his place for the following game at Belle Vue, again finding the net in a 2–1 defeat to Swansea, but Rovers struggled badly and Kitchen returned to the reserves before returning to play a part in the final 8 games, scoring 4 goals in the process. Things were looking good for him to become a regular in the side, but the team were relegated and McMenemy replaced as manager by Maurice Setters. Kitchen was seemingly back to square one as he made only 6 starts the following year.

He started the 1972 season as a regular in the team and despite Rovers managing only 1 point from the first 6 games, Kitchen had already helped himself to a couple of goals. The following season began with more optimism, a number of players had joined Kitchen in the first team from the club's youth set up, and big striker Brendan O'Callaghan joined the Rovers forward line. He and Kitchen immediately hit it off with O'Callaghan's ability in the air a constant source of ammunition for the ever-alert Kitchen. The pair scored 26 goals between them including 2 at Anfield in the memorable draw with the eventual FA Cup winners that would have seen Rovers produce one of the biggest upsets ever had Kitchen's late effort found the net instead of the crossbar.

The next few years saw Kitchen's talents blossom alongside O'Callaghan and winger Ian Miller; the trio were an exciting unit to watch and guaranteed goals with Kitchen scoring over 20 in the league for the next three seasons. The only black spot was that despite the talent and goals the team possessed, they never managed to achieve promotion, leaving Kitchen frustrated and keen to test himself at a higher level. He spent most of his final season with the club on the transfer list, before moving to Second Division Leyton Orient in the summer for £45,000.

He proved he could score goals at a higher level, even in a struggling Orient side, and dragged the team to the semi-finals of the FA Cup, scoring 7 of the team's 9 goals in the competition. He went on to play for Fulham (moving for £150,000) and Cardiff before heading back to Orient (via a spell in Hong Kong) where he was again among the goals during a career which saw over 150 league goals.

The only mystery sounding the career of Peter Kitchen was how he never got the opportunity to play at the highest level. Although not the quickest of strikers, he was razor-sharp in the penalty box and he was a supreme finisher – but his game offered more than just goals. He came alive in the box, often needing only one touch where others would've needed two. He scored 101 goals for the club and is a genuine Rovers legend.

Brendan O'Callaghan

Brendan enjoyed a fantastic pairing with striker Peter Kitchen in the 1970s and the two perfectly complemented each other with Kitchen alive to the inevitable flicks bestowed to him by the powerful big front man. O'Callaghan not only made chances for others, but was also more than capable of finishing them off himself and is still considered by many to be the best target man to have ever played for the club.

Born in Bradford on 23 July 1955 he made his professional debut against his hometown Bradford City for the Rovers in September 1973 at just 18. Standing 6ft 2in tall, he went on to terrorise defences alongside Kitchen and winger Ian Miller throughout the 1970s with many notable games along the way including a great hat-trick (again back in Bradford), and the side's epic League Cup run in 1975. This saw O'Callaghan scoring 6 times in 7 outings on the way to a memorable quarter-final away at Tottenham, Rovers taking the lead early on before Spurs eventually ran out 7–2 winners with the team still very much in the game until late on.

Indeed, as with Kitchen, the only black spot was that O'Callaghan's time at the club was exclusively in the fourth tier of English football, with defensive weaknesses meaning the side at the time never managed to amount to the true sum of its parts. During 1975/76 O'Callaghan and Kitchen both netted 22 league goals apiece (an incredible feat not seen since by a Rovers strike partnership) in a team which scored 75 goals during the term but also contrived to concede 69. It was this failure to progress in the league which ultimately meant the break-up of the side with Kitchen leaving first to try the test of a higher tier. In March 1978 Brendan moved to Second Division Stoke City for £40,000 where his goals gained the Potters promotion to the top fight. He showed himself more than capable of playing on such a grand stage against the top sides in the country, contributing significantly to the side and constantly leading the line. He switched to centre-half late on in his career, with equal assurance and efficiency, before a brief stint at Oldham and prior to ending his career in 1985.

In total he played 212 times for the Rovers, scoring 74 goals and making countless more along the way. Fondly remembered by the fans, he played a full part in a thoroughly entertaining and exciting period in the history of the club.

Ian Miller

Ian Miller joined the Rovers from Forest and was to prove a key figure in the team's midfield. Born in Perth, Scotland, in May 1955, 'Windy' started his football career as an apprentice at Bury in August 1973 making his league debut during the 1973/74 season. He started just 9 times for the Shakers before his potential was spotted by Nottingham Forest and he was taken to the City Ground. He spent a year at Forest and despite not playing for the first team, his time by the Trent was certainly not wasted as Brian Clough's influence undoubtedly made him a better footballer. He joined Doncaster in the summer of 1975. That first year he quickly became an integral part of a pacy, exciting Rovers side that scored its highest number of goals for ten years. Miller supplied the ammunition that O'Callaghan and Kitchen fired on their way to 22 league goals apiece, and he helped himself to 9 all of his own on his way to pipping both players to the supporters' Player of the Year, an honour he went on to win again the following year – no mean feat among such distinguished company.

Miller went on to join Swindon in 1978 as the team broke up before going to enjoy a successful spell in the Second Division with Blackburn Rovers, making 252 league appearances for the side before ending his career with spells at Port Vale and Scunthorpe.

A lightning quick winger, he was a tricky dribbler and great crosser of the ball. He was a third a of Rovers' 'holy trinity' with the enduring thought of the era being that Miller would beat 'em down the wing, cross to O'Callaghan to beat 'em in the air, for Kitchen to turn on a sixpence and score during a time when the side regularly played fast, attacking football to the enjoyment of the crowd.

TOP CUP RUNS

League Cup 1975/76
The season was a decent one for the Rovers, finishing 10th in Division Four, but really the side had enough to have finished much higher and it was the League Cup which proved to be the evidence that the side contained some real quality.

Rovers drew Third Division Grimsby Town and thanks to a superb display (inspired by a Brendan O'Callaghan hat-trick) in the first leg, the Rovers moved through to a second round tie, once again against a side from a division above. Crystal Palace had started the season superbly and were unbeaten before their visit to Belle Vue – however, they could never recover as Rovers went ahead early to end the Eagles' run.

Next up would be a difficult trip all the way to Torquay which needed a terrific fight back from the Rovers and a late equaliser to force a replay, where a brilliant display sent them through to the last sixteen of the competition for the very first time. Hull City were the visitors, playing two tiers above the Rovers in Division Two, attracting a crowd of over 20,000. Peter Kitchen did what he did best and put the Rovers ahead before Hull equalised and began to take control of the game. Some resolute defending and some fine saves from keeper Denis Peacock kept the Tigers out and Ray Ternent produced a fine diving header to see the Rovers to a splendid victory, and the quarter-finals.

The reward was a trip to White Hart Lane to play a Spurs team which had won the competition outright in two of the previous five years. Undaunted, the Rovers had the front to take the lead before Spurs hit back to lead 2–1 at half time. Peter Kitchen again popped up just after half time to level at 2–2 and the travelling Rovers fans were beginning to dream of what might be. Unfortunately, an own goal from captain Chappell put Spurs back in front and the dream was over, with Spurs flooding forward to eventually win the game 7–2. The one-sided scoreline did not do justice to another excellent performance, worthy of such a wonderful cup run.

First Round first leg, 20 August 1975
Doncaster Rovers   3–1   Grimsby Town
O'Callaghan (3)
Rovers: Peacock, Reed, Ternent, Chappell, Uzelac, Brookes, Curran, Alesinoye, O'Callaghan, Kitchen, Higgins. Sub: Wignall for Alesinoye.
Attendance: 3,218

First Round second leg, 25 August 1975
Grimsby Town   0–0   Doncaster Rovers
Rovers: Peacock, Reed, Ternent, Chappell, Uzelac, Brookes, Curran, Alesinoye, O'Callaghan, Kitchen, Higgins.
Attendance: 5,552

Second Round, 9 September 1975
Doncaster Rovers   2–1   Crystal Palace
Chappell
O'Callaghan
Rovers: Peacock, Reed, Robinson, Chappell, Uzelac,
Brookes, Miller, Alesinoye, O'Callaghan, Kitchen,
Balderstone.
Attendance: 6,268

Third Round, 8 October 1975
Torquay United   1–1   Doncaster Rovers
                                Reed
Rovers: Peacock, Reed, Robinson, Chappell, Uzelac,
Brookes, Miller, Murray, O'Callaghan, Kitchen,
Balderstone.
Attendance: 2,785

Third Round replay, 13 October 1975
Doncaster Rovers   3–0   Torquay United
O'Callaghan (2)
Balderstone
Rovers: Peacock, Reed, Robinson, Chappell, Uzelac,
Brookes, Miller, Murray, O'Callaghan, Kitchen,
Balderstone.
Attendance: 9,784

Fourth Round, 11 November 1975
Doncaster Rovers   2–1   Hull City
Kitchen
Ternent
Rovers: Peacock, Reed, Robinson, Ternent, Uzelac, Brookes,
Miller, Murray, O'Callaghan, Kitchen, Balderstone.
Attendance: 20,476

Fifth Round, 3 December 1975
Tottenham Hotspur   7–2   Doncaster Rovers
                               Murray
                               Kitchen
Rovers: Peacock, Reed, Robinson, Chappell, Uzelac,
Brookes, Miller, Murray, O'Callaghan, Kitchen,
Balderstone.
Attendance: 25,702

KIT HISTORY

The club's home colours are famously red and white, but
the first strip ever worn by Doncaster Rovers in 1879 was
blue and white. The navy blue shirt had a yellow diagonal
cross emblazoned across the front and was worn with white
shorts and navy socks.

The first kit worn as a League club was a solid red shirt
with black trim and black socks, but the design has varied
ever since, though it has always been solid red or white
shirts or red and white hoops or stripes.

In 2001 Rovers reverted to red and white hoops as this
was seen to have been worn during their most successful
eras in the past. This has remained the familiar design ever
since – what appeared to be a superstitious move turned out
to be a wise one following the dramatic upturn in the club's
fortunes.

The first shirt sponsors were seen in 1982 when CIL
agreed a 2-year sponsorship deal with the club and shirt
sponsorship has remained with the club, as with the rest of
football, ever since.

DREAM DEBUTS

Northern Irish forward Tommy Aiken made his debut for the Rovers on 2 December 1967 in a league match against Halifax Town, having just signed for the club from Ballymena United. It didn't take Aiken long to make an impression with his new club, as he nipped in to score after only 6½ seconds – a supreme effort which still remains as one of the fastest ever scored in the Football League.

David 'Bruno' Jones signed for the Rovers in early November 1989 with the club struggling near the foot of the Football League having won only 2 of their 16 league games during the season. Jones lined up with his new team-mates on 11 November 1989 and went on to notch a superb hat-trick as Rovers beat Rochdale 3–1 away. It was a dream debut for the striker and set Rovers on a run of 5 wins over the next 6 games which turned the season around.

MIKE BASSETT, DONCASTER PLAYER

Ricky Tomlinson's fictional film character, bumbling England manager Mike Bassett, is said to have played for Doncaster in 1975. This is affirmed by Mike's wife who states, 'I first met Mike in 1975, when he was with Crewe Alexandra, and he was at loan from Doncaster at the time so I remember thinking they might ask for him back, luckily Doncaster told Crewe they could keep him.'

MANAGERIAL GREATS – SEAN O'DRISCOLL

Following a successful playing career which began at Fulham and then moved to Bournemouth and included over 550 appearances (his 423 appearances for Bournemouth was, until recently, a club record) and 3 international caps for the Republic of Ireland, Sean O'Driscoll joined the Cherries coaching staff following his retirement in 1995, and went on to manage the youth team before being installed in charge of the first team in 2000. On an extremely limited budget, he created a team which was far superior to the sum of its parts at Dean Court. They played a good quality brand of football which was able to provide the club with some success as O'Driscoll guided the side to victory at the Millennium Stadium in Cardiff and promotion to Division Two via the play-offs in 2003.

His Bournemouth side continued to punch above its weight against a backdrop of ever worsening financial problems, and when John Ryan was looking for a replacement for the departed Dave Penney in 2006, he looked to the South Coast. O'Driscoll had caught the eye of the Rovers chairman previously when his Bournemouth side comprehensively beat the Rovers in impressive style. After 23 years associated with Bournemouth, O'Driscoll headed to South Yorkshire in the knowledge that he would have more resources available, but increased expectation from a club which was thirsty for Championship football.

That season he was able to guide the club to its first major cup final, winning the Football League Trophy (and earning the distinction of having managed two teams to victory there) in one of the biggest days in the club's history, but not before he encountered something of a slow start. His reign started with a number of draws and little in the way of goals or free-flowing, attacking football and led to a number of supporters questioning his appointment almost immediately. However, he was named manager of the month in January and as the club enjoyed its JP Trophy run, O'Driscoll seemed to have begun to put his own stamp on the side. At the beginning of his first full season in charge, he broke the club's record transfer fee by paying £200,000 to secure the signature of striker James Hayter from former side Bournemouth.

His Rovers side finished third in League One in 2007/08 and qualified for the play-offs, despite having been in pole position to gain automatic promotion as late as the final day of the season. The play-off semi-final demolition of Southend underlined the side's reputation for playing attractive, attacking football and the subsequent 1–0 win over Leeds United in the final at Wembley saw Rovers win promotion back to the second tier for the first time in over 50 years, handing the club the biggest day in its history.

His reputation enhanced further, the side made a good start to life in the Championship before struggling badly. Bottom of the league at Christmas and struggling for goals, O'Driscoll persevered with his football philosophy and suddenly results began to match performances. The club went on a superb run finishing comfortably in mid-table, with further progression the following year when the side were play-off contenders for much of the season. They found goals much easier to come by, having learned important lessons from the previous year. They adopted a more varied style of play, allowing the option of going more direct, allied with maintaining the high standards of football and short passing game O'Driscoll demands from his side.

Sometimes a little cautious when his team gets ahead, O'Driscoll has not been without criticism during his reign as manager, but his achievements have been undoubtedly among the best any Rovers manager has attained. His growing reputation for playing a superb 'pass and move' style of football which has consistently earned Rovers plaudits from all areas of football has not gone unnoticed and O'Driscoll has been linked to a number of higher-profile positions.

A manager with a relaxed and laid-back character, he is arguably more concerned with the quality of his side's performance than the final score, and has created a Rovers team which makes the most of the personnel available to it. Despite living with limited resources in relation to its peers, his Rovers team has probably overachieved, and is now capable of accomplishing great things.

	Played	Won	Lost	Drawn
2006–11*	259	96	92	71

*prior to 2011/12 season

MOST EXPENSIVE TEAM EVER BOUGHT

Below is a team made up of the club's most expensive signings, playing in a 4-4-3 formation. The starting eleven ranges from £50,000 to over £1 million, and is made up of various players whose success at the club has been just as varied. The combined cost of the club's premier eleven is £2,452,500.

Alan Blayney	£50k	Billy Sharp	£1.15m
James O'Connor	£130k	James Hayter	£200k
John Philliben	£60k	Subs	
Darren Moore	£62.5k	Gk. Gary O'Connor	£25k
Matt Mills	£300k	Def. Russ Wilcox	£60k
Sean Thornton	£175k	Def. Graeme Lee	£50k
Brian Stock	£150k	Mid. Dean Shiels	£50k
Michael McIndoe	£50k	Att. Justin Jackson	£100k
Paul Heffernan	£125k		

THEY SAID IT

'I got the rub of the green.'
Teessider James Coppinger, following his breathtaking hat-trick against Southend in the League One play-off semi-final

'It's not a day out: if we wanted that we could buy tickets for a Wembley tour. This is work. Southend is over, finished, but if my players need any more motivation for this game, they're wasting their time being footballers. We've tried to keep things simple this week, because the bigger the game the more you have to retain the basics. We're the underdogs and we'll have fewer fans, but at the end of this game, we just want to be able to say we've achieved something.'
Sean O'Driscoll tries to remain the only calm man in Doncaster ahead of the Wembley clash with Leeds United

'The club is looking to go forward. The chairman is very ambitious and can get a bit carried away at times. He wants us to win the Champions League next year but I have told him we have to get into the Premier League first.'
Richard O'Kelly on working for Chairman John Ryan

'I'm surprised I even hit it, my legs were like jelly!'
After five years in the Conference, one goal took Rovers back into the league. The man who scored the goal was Francis Tierney

FOOTBALL'S 'OVERACHIEVERS'

In October 2008 the new Football Pools published *The achievers report*. Its aim was to put each of the 92 English Football League clubs on an equal footing in order to measure each club's performance from 1992 (this was the year the Premier League was introduced and the subsequent new Football League structure was established). The report calculated each club's position from a number of criteria including their standings at the start of the study in 1992, average attendances and stadium capacity, financial ownership, investment and difficulties as well as dealings in the transfer market, and perhaps most importantly, league and cup performances.

And so it was that Doncaster Rovers were crowned overachievers extraordinaire by the report. Topping the list, the club was deemed to be 'pound for pound' the top performing club in English football, comfortably ahead of the likes of Manchester United, Arsenal, Chelsea and Liverpool. Rovers were awarded the title having risen from twenty-first in the Fourth Division at the end of the 1991/92 season to line up in the Championship in 2008. In addition, Rovers endured a spell of severe mismanagement and decline, where attendances fell below the 2,000 mark. The club's then chairman was sent to prison for conspiring to burn the Main Stand down, and the club spent 5 years trying to regain its League status following relegation to the Conference. It's little wonder really then, that Rovers should rightly take their place, and some much deserved acclaim on top of English football!

ROVERS GREATS – 1980s

Ian Snodin

Ian's career with the Rovers really saw everything. Making his debut at 17 years old, he became club captain two years later while still a teenager (and at the time the youngest captain in the entire Football League) and he represented England at under-21 and under-23 levels while at Belle Vue. He won promotion with the club twice under manager Billy Bremner and returned nearly twenty years later as manager, to help guide the club back from extinction.

Ian is probably one of the most naturally gifted players to wear the Rovers shirt in the modern era. His ability on the ball, with his superb vision and range of passing, allied with an unbreakable never-say-die attitude and a willingness to run and run, made him a true hero on the Belle Vue terraces.

He made his debut as a substitute on 29 March 1980 and within 6 months became a regular in a Rovers side that won promotion from Division Four in 1981. He went on to captain the side which was once again promoted to Division Three in 1984 and it was following this that Ian enjoyed probably his best year for the club, missing only 4 league games as Rovers became a competitive force in the Third Division. Inevitably Ian moved onwards and upwards, joining Leeds United in the summer of 1985 for £200,000, money that cash-strapped Rovers could not turn down.

Ian became captain at Leeds United before his performances led to a move into the First Division when Everton paid out £840,000 to secure his signature. He moved to one of the most successful sides of the period, with whom he won the championship.

A switch to full-back proved extremely successful and Ian was rewarded with a call-up to the England squad, though unfortunately injury forced his withdrawal and hampered his progress from then on. He spent time on loan with Sunderland before moving to Oldham and then a short spell at Scarborough before teaming up with brother Glynn as manager at Rovers. The club had just been relegated from the Football League and had been facing almost certain extinction before John Ryan bought the club and installed one of the club's most famous sons at the helm. With only a handful of players and not much else, Ian helped rebuild the club and managed a mid-table finish before winning the Conference trophy in front of a sold-out Belle Vue in a brief welcome return to former glories. Ian Snodin made 222 appearances for the club, scoring 29 goals, and is still remembered with great affection at the club.

Glynn Snodin

A key figure in Bremner's side at the time and during Rovers' success over the next few seasons was undoubtedly Glynn Snodin. A left-sided midfielder who could also play at full-back, Glynn overcame a shaky start to his Rovers career as a 16-year-old to become a Belle Vue favourite, with his whole-hearted attitude and 100 per cent commitment earning him the adulation of the Rovers fans. Glynn had a great left foot, possessing a powerful shot, and he would often let fly whenever the chance arose. He scored some spectacular goals during his career including a great strike in a game away at Darlington and one crucial drive at home to Bradford as Rovers chased promotion in 1981. Glynn actually finished as Rovers' top scorer twice while at the club. A consistent performer and excellent professional, Glynn made 340 appearances for the club (many of which were alongside brother Ian) scoring 61 goals before moving to Sheffield Wednesday in June 1985 for a large fee for the time which was in excess of £100,000, spending two years at Wednesday before joining up with Ian again at Leeds. He also spent time at Oldham, Rotherham and Hearts before ending his playing career at Barnsley in 1993. After this Glynn completed his coaching qualifications and turned down the chance to become assistant manager at Oakwell in 1998 to rejoin Rovers as assistant to Ian, taking on the seemingly impossible task of rebuilding the club following relegation to the Conference as the brothers made the first crucial steps to setting the club back on the path to success. Following their departure in 2000, Glynn joined Charlton as reserve team boss. Now a hugely respected and talented coach, Glynn worked with former Charlton colleague Alan Curbishley at Premier League West Ham United.

Alan Warboys

A central figure at the club for a spell in the early 1980s was striker/centre-half Alan Warboys. Warboys, who grew up in Goldthorpe, Barnsley, was an apprentice at the Rovers before signing professional forms in 1967, making his debut during the same month and scoring his first league goal a couple of weeks later against Scunthorpe. He was perhaps never the most gifted of footballers, but what he lacked in ability he more than compensated for with endeavour, making him a crowd favourite at Belle Vue and at Sheffield Wednesday whom he joined in June 1968.

Warboys enjoyed prolific spells at Cardiff and Bristol Rovers with a brief stay at Sheffield United in between. In February 1977 he joined Fulham where he played with some quality players who included Rodney Marsh, Bobby Moore and George Best before finding his way back to Doncaster via Hull in 1979 and promptly won the player of the season accolade back at Belle Vue. Warboys was a hard-working, true professional who made 149 appearances in two spells for the club, scoring 36 goals before struggling with a back injury which ultimately ended his career in 1982.

THE TONY COLEMAN STORY

On 6 May 1966 Rovers entertained Notts County in a game they were desperate to win in order to further progress their march towards promotion with only three games remaining. Things didn't go well on that night at Belle Vue; Rovers struggled to get going and were frustrated by a number of 'questionable' decisions awarded against them by referee Mr Jack Pickles, with a number of them serving to frustrate the home side's talented midfielder Tony Coleman.

Coleman fell victim to a number of niggling and cynical fouls in the middle of the pitch that continually went unchecked by the obstinate Pickles and his frustration was beginning to grow as each moment ticked by. Coleman's mood was clearly not helped by his side's performance, as with 15 minutes to go the home side were 3–0 down and lucky to have registered nil. It was at this point that County winger Tony Flower had yet another 'coming together' with Coleman which again went unpunished by the match official, and proved the straw which broke the camel's back. Coleman stood up, the ball long since gone, and booted the visiting midfielder as if he was trying to kick him onto the Main Stand roof, leaving him lying on the Belle Vue turf. Mr Pickles immediately showed he was in possession of some cards that evening should he feel inclined to use them, and promptly gave Coleman his marching orders.

After setting off on the lonely walk to the dressing room, Coleman appeared to think better of it, turned round and proceeded to punch the referee squarely in the head. Players from both sides were needed to separate the two and Coleman eventually left the field, to receive the backing of his chairman, who vowed to support one of his star players in any inquiry into the incident.

Inquiry there was, but it is now universally accepted that the referee swore at Coleman as he left the pitch and this prompted his about turn and subsequent Muhammad Ali impression. As a result the FA adopted a lenient approach to his punishment, handing out only a 6-week ban!

Loved by Rovers fans even before the incident, Coleman became a hero on the Belle Vue terraces as a result of it. He left Rovers to enjoy a richly distinguished career, with the hard man winning the Fourth Division with Rovers that year and going on to win the League Championship and FA Cup with Manchester City.

TOP NICKNAMES

'Sumo' Gary Brabin
Stan 'Dizzy' Burton
Colin 'Duggie' Douglas
Ian 'Windy' Miller
David 'Bruno' Jones
Peter 'Kitch' Kitchen
Albert 'Yogi' Broadbent
Colin 'Baresi' Cramb
Colin 'Psycho' Sutherland
'Mental' Mickey Norbury
Mark 'Sarge' Albrighton
Ricky 'Red Card' Ravenhill
Jason 'Afro Goal Machine' Price

HAT-TRICK OF SAVES

During the early 1990s, the Rovers visited Spotland to play Rochdale in a Fourth Division encounter. The game will be forever remembered for the amazing contribution Paul Crichton provided.

The referee awarded the home side something of a contentious penalty so Rovers clearly felt that justice had been done when keeper Crichton made a fantastic full-length dive to turn the spot-kick away, only for the referee to order a retake. Somewhat baffled, Crichton again lined up for the penalty, and again made an excellent stop to keep the ball out, only for the referee to wave the Rovers' players protests away and once again signalled for the penalty to be retaken.

Visibly angered and aggrieved, the Rovers shot-stopper unbelievably produced a third outstanding penalty save to the total amazement of everyone present – including the referee, who by this point dare not stop the game for a fourth time and allowed play to continue!

GREATEST GAMES

Rovers 3–2 Bristol Rovers, 1 April 2007
1 April 2007 saw the club play its first major cup final in its long history, and 18,000 Rovers fans made the trip to Cardiff's Millennium Stadium for the Football League Trophy final against Bristol Rovers. Doncaster were favourites going into the game, playing a division above their opponents, but Bristol Rovers were going well in League Two and had yet to concede a goal in the trophy, having beaten some good sides to take their place in the final.

Doncaster were given a massive boost before kick off when forward Jason Price and top scorer Paul Heffernan were passed fit to play, with Heffernan having been absent for the previous 7 games with an ankle injury. Heffernan was the club's top marksman and had been the hero of the two-legged semi-final, scoring four goals as the team edged past Crewe in a nail-biting match. The Irishman's inclusion in the final served as a huge lift for all.

The Cardiff pitch was bathed in sun on a crisp Sunday afternoon with half of its imposing and impressive stadium bathed in red and white and both teams were keen to get off to a good start. Inside the first minute, Price fizzed the ball in towards Heffernan in the box. He challenged two defenders and got a foot to the ball just before keeper Phillips, and the ball spun straight to Jonathan Forte who had the simple task of rolling the ball into an empty net. It was a dream start to the final, and just what manager Sean O'Driscoll would have wanted to settle his team down. Within minutes, things would get even better.

The Doncaster fans were still celebrating the opening goal when keeper Neil Sullivan sent a long goal-kick down field. Heffernan was alive to it, as the ball bounced over the Bristol Rovers back four, and he latched onto the loose ball before firing home a superb left-footed shot down into the far corner of the net for his 21st goal of the season. The watching fans could hardly believe what they were seeing as their team cruised to a 2-goal advantage.

The game then started to settle down and a shell-shocked Bristol Rovers managed to get hold of the ball and attempt to play their way back into the game. Midfielder Lewis Haldane tested Neil Sullivan with an angled drive, but the Rovers keeper made a comfortable save and neither team looked likely to add to the scoring as the half drew to a close.

Bristol Rovers started the second half brightly, looking for an early goal of their own to drag them back into the game – and within 4 minutes of the restart they did just that. Walker whipped a low cross in from the left-hand side and Rovers defender Sean McDaid stepped across midfielder Sammy Igoe to let the ball run to safety. In doing so the referee adjudged he had fouled the Bristol Rovers man and Walker placed the resultant penalty past Sullivan.

Heffernan had a snap shot from a Coppinger pass blocked as Rovers looked to restore their advantage, the game starting to open up. But, just beyond the hour mark Igoe latched onto the ball 7 yards from goal following good work down the left and swept the ball home to level the scores.

The momentum now with them, Bristol Rovers charged forward in search of a winner with Haldane and Walker both going close before Doncaster went close themselves with skipper Graeme Lee having a shot blocked on the line, Brian Stock firing the rebound wide. Paul Green went close with a late header before Paul Heffernan shot wide with a chance to win the game in the final minute. It was a breathtaking end to the 90 minutes as the game spilled into 30 minutes' extra time.

Steve Elliott headed the first chance of the extra period straight at Sullivan and Green went close at the other end as Doncaster began to look the most likely to score. With only 10 minutes remaining, Lee found room in the 6-yard box to nod home the winner from a Sean Thornton corner as the Doncaster fans erupted once more. The side held out, and Lee himself held the trophy aloft amid a backdrop of fireworks and fantastic celebrations.

KEEPMOAT'S NUMBER ONE

Barbados international striker Mark McCammon holds the honour of being the first player to score at the Keepmoat Stadium. The big striker scored (quite a notable achievement in itself for a striker who only managed a handful of goals throughout his time at the club) the first goal after only 9 minutes in Rovers' 3–0 victory over Huddersfield Town on New Year's Day 2007 to christen the stadium perfectly.

MANAGERIAL GREATS – BILLY BREMNER

Billy Bremner was undoubtedly one of the finest players of his generation. He was the heartbeat of both the Scotland national team and the all-conquering Leeds United team of the 1960s and '70s, with whom he won every domestic honour the English game has to offer.

In November 1978, Stan Anderson resigned as Doncaster Rovers manager, with the club among the bottom places of the Football League. Five days later the club appointed a born winner and leader into Anderson's place and gave Billy Bremner his first managerial role.

Bremner dragged the club up by its bootstraps with his demand for hard work and passion sending a new dose of pride surging through the club. Rovers improved under his guidance and he brought through a core of talented teenagers, introducing names such as Daral Pugh, Steve Lister and Glynn Snodin to the rigours of professional football. But if the Scot had been looking for a young player in his own likeness, he soon found one in Ian Snodin. He clearly saw the talent the young midfielder possessed and handed him his full senior debut at just 16 and made him captain at 18 years of age.

Bremner produced a team which was desperate to play for him, wanted to win for him, and would have run through a solid wall at his say-so. This Bremner-inspired hard work and desire, allied with no little measure of ability, saw the team promoted in 1981. Following a great start to the season, they won all 6 games in September as Bremner was named manager of the month; the side pushed on in the New Year and were promoted following a run of 3 wins in the final 5 games.

Two years in Division Three were ended in 1983 when, despite some early goal feasts producing great wins (a 6–1 win v Exeter and 7–5 thriller against Reading), the side struggled as players moved on and injuries took their toll, meaning a terrible second half to the season ended with relegation.

The club was now a different animal, and Bremner, with some shrewd additions to the playing staff, inspired the team to bounce straight back and win promotion at the first attempt. These achievements had not gone unnoticed, however, and in October 1985 Leeds United came calling with an offer that Bremner could not refuse.

He returned to Rovers in the summer of 1989 and found the club experiencing deep financial problems. On the pitch the team struggled before Bremner made some key signings while still operating within the club's stiflingly tight financial budget, and he once again lifted Rovers up the league and, amazingly, to within one game of a Wembley cup final, narrowly missing out to Tranmere Rovers in the Leyland DAF Trophy over two legs.

Bremner made some further, crucial free transfer signings and the following season, the team which were now made up of his own players, set off like a train, equalling a club record in winning the first 5 league games.

Rovers were top, heading into the New Year, but once again financial difficulties meant that key players were sold and injuries played their part on an ever-depleting squad (at one point Rovers had eight first team players missing through injury or suspension) and the side dropped down the division, eventually missing out on even a play-off place.

Bremner's teams always played an attacking, passing brand of football that tried to play 'the right way'. His Rovers teams were built on a foundation of togetherness and team spirit and a sense of everyone being 'in it together'.

Arguably not the greatest coach, Bremner was a fantastic motivator whose passion for the game spread throughout the whole club. He achieved a great deal over his two spells at Rovers under difficult circumstances, and for his achievements and the advances he made off the field, he is surely one of the club's greatest ever managers.

	Played	Won	Lost	Drawn
1978–85	320	115	122	83

	Played	Won	Lost	Drawn
1989–91	116	33	54	29

	Played	Won	Lost	Drawn
Total	436	148	176	112

TUESDAY AFTERNOON FOOTBALL

In March 1992 the Rovers (as they so often were in the 1990s) were fighting for their lives at the bottom of the Fourth Division. Barnet, competing at the other end of the table, were due at Belle Vue for a Tuesday night game as the side looked to battle against the odds for a crucial 3 points. The uphill battle for survival seemed even steeper when the floodlights at Belle Vue were damaged prior to the game which meant the night kick off couldn't possibly go ahead. Looking for a solution so the game could proceed, the Rovers set a new 'daylight' kick off time of 5pm, only for the police to scupper their plans due to the clash with the rush hour traffic through the town. Barnsley were the next to come up with a solution, but their offer to provide use of Oakwell was rejected by the Football League, leaving the club with no option but to play the game at 2 o'clock in the afternoon. Cash-strapped Rovers braced themselves for their lowest attendance, but 1,247 skipped work or school to make it to Belle Vue to see the game 'that nearly never was'. They were glad they did too, as Mike Jeffrey's first-half goal was enough to see Rovers home 1–0 and helped, ultimately, steer the club to safety.

DISASTERS ...

The 2002/03 season will be forever remembered with great fondness by all Rovers fans as the year the club escaped the Conference and rejoined the elite among the Football League. However, not many fans recall that the season began with something of a wobble.

With the season still in its infancy, Rovers headed to Telford as strong favourites for the 3 points, a position that was further enhanced by a blistering first-half display which saw Rovers, courtesy of goals from Dave Morley, Dean Barrick and 2 from Fran Tierney, 4–0 up after 32 minutes. In complete control of the game, it didn't matter that Telford snatched 2 consolation goals in the second half as the home side were reduced to 10 men with only 8 minutes to go ... Cue the obligatory disaster. Somehow, the side that had been in complete control of the game throughout, decided to throw their advantage away to the 10 men and only just managed to escape with a point, with the visiting Rovers fans looking on in dumbfounded disbelief as their team managed to hold on for a 4–4 draw!

TOP CUP RUNS

Football Conference Trophy, 1998/99
While admittedly not the highest profile or most auspicious trophy to win, set against the background of the 1998/99 season the victory in the final was celebrated at Belle Vue with as much passion and pride as any of the top cup competitions.

Having completed the club's first season in the Conference, avoiding a second relegation and still being in existence was cause for celebration enough and the Conference Trophy signalled a new beginning for the club, offering hope, and a glimpse of what might still be in the future. It also offered a vehicle for a huge expression of pride in a team who had started the season with nothing. Rebuilding from both relegation from the Football League and the Ken Richardson era, the management team of Ian and Glynn Snodin had given the town a football team which they could be proud of once again.

The second leg of the final at Belle Vue was played in front of a packed-out home crowd of 7,160, with the terraces a sea of red and white, evoking memories of more successful times in the club's history.

The game itself was a pretty one-sided affair, with the Rovers, already 1–0 ahead from the first leg, taking an early lead when Colin Sutherland turned to fire home from inside the 6-yard box.

The home side settled into the game and Ian Duerden headed home in fine style following a well-worked move down the right-hand side to effectively end the tie before half time. Duerden added a third in the second period with a superb long-range finish to win the tie with a comprehensive 4–0 aggregate victory.

Skipper Dave Penney climbed the steps in the Main Stand at Belle Vue to be presented with the trophy, in front of the Rovers fans who had amassed on the pitch in a scene which was to be one of the defining and most enduring moments in the modern history of the football club.

Second Round, 1 December 1998
Doncaster Rovers   2–0   Southport
Hume (2)
Rovers: Woods, George, Shaw, Ybarra, Warren, Sutherland, Maamria, Jones, Duerden, Hume, Beckett.
Subs: Powell, Wild, Ridley.
Attendance: 949

Third Round, 2 March 1999
Doncaster Rovers   3–2   Northwich Victoria
Barnwell-Edinboro (2)
George
Rovers: Woods, Ybarra, Caudwell, Nicol, George, Beckett,
Penney, Cunningham, Duerden, Barnwell-Edinboro,
Maamria. Subs: Jones, Powell, Wild.
Attendance: 1,877

Semi-final, first leg, 30 March 1999
Morecambe   1–2   Doncaster Rovers
                                   Duerden (2)
Rovers: Woods, Minett, Caudwell, Foster, Warren,
Sutherland, Watson, Goodwin, Duerden, Kirkwood,
Maxfield. Subs: Penney, Barnwell-Edinboro, George.
Attendance: 1,302

Semi-final, second leg, 8 April 1999
Doncaster Rovers   1–0   Morecambe
Watson
Rovers: Woods, Minett, Shaw, Warren, Penney, Sutherland,
Watson, Foster, Duerden, Kirkwood, Beckett. Subs:
Barnwell-Edinboro, Hume, George.
Attendance: 3,297

Final, first Leg, 20 April 1999
Farnborough Town   0–1   Doncaster Rovers
                                   Penney
Rovers: Woods, Shaw, Maxfield, Warren, Penney,
Sutherland, Watson, Goodwin, Duerden, Kirkwood,
Minett. Subs: Foster, Barnwell-Edinboro, Caudwell.
Attendance: 643

Final, second leg, 3 May 1999
Doncaster Rovers   3–0   Farnborough Town
Sutherland
Duerden (2)
Rovers: Woods, Shaw, Maxfield, Warren, Penney,
Sutherland, Minett, Goodwin, Duerden, Barnwell-
Edinboro, Watson. Subs: Caudwell, Kirkwood, Foster.
Attendance: 7,160

THE TUNNELS OF BELLE VUE

Belle Vue was once the only Football League grounds to have
separate tunnels for the home and away players to come out
onto the pitch and enter the changing rooms from, with even
a third tunnel in place to provide access for ground staff.

WHEN GAZZA PLAYED FOR ROVERS

On 7 May 1990, Paul Gascoigne appeared at Belle Vue in a
Rovers shirt. The midfielder turned out for a Rovers XI in
a testimonial match for former goalkeeper Paul Malcolm
whose career was ended by injury. Gazza scored a hat-trick
as the Rovers beat Barnsley 7–3, and also hit the crossbar
from the half way line, before delighting the crowd by
trapping a cross-field pass stone dead – with his backside!
The game took place just weeks before he became a world
star following his performances for England at the 1990
World Cup and it is to his eternal credit he took the time to
appear at Belle Vue.

WHERE'S THE BLUE?

During the club's Football League career Rovers have played against and beaten some top teams such as Manchester United, Liverpool, Arsenal and Manchester City. Strangely, of all the 'big boys' of English Football, the Rovers have never come up against Chelsea.

ROVERS GREATS – 1990s

Colin Cramb
Colin joined the Rovers in December 1995 for a reported £25,000. Still only 21, he had begun his career at Hamilton where he was considered one of Scotland's brightest prospects after scoring twice on his debut as a 16-year-old. Moves to English Premier League side Southampton and Scottish Premier clubs Falkirk and Hearts followed, but the talented striker never really established himself at that level and joined a Rovers team going well, and in the Third Division play-off places.

Signed as a strike partner to the club's leading scorer Graeme Jones, Cramb immediately settled into the role, and his ability to bring others into play with some quality touches helped Rovers to a 4–1 win on his debut. Inevitably, the club's promotion challenge faltered but Cramb showed his worth scoring 7 times in 20 league games.

The following season saw Cramb feature as the club's leading striker with Jones having moved on, and the Scot delivered the goals that were expected from him, finding the net 21 times in all competitions, which included 18 league goals. This made him the first Rovers player to break the 20-goal barrier for some 20 years.

With the club struggling financially, Cramb became one of a number of key first team players to leave during the summer of 1997 with a £125,000 move to Bristol City serving as his reward for such a fruitful season among the goals. He enjoyed promotion at Ashton Gate before a £200,000 move to Crewe. He subsequently played in Holland with Fortuna Sittard before returning with spells at Shrewsbury and Grimsby, moving back to Hamilton in 2005. He also enjoyed successful times with Stenhousemuir, Stirling and East Stirlingshire before retiring in 2009 having scored well over 100 goals.

His goals made him a big favourite with the Belle Vue crowd, providing them with a goalscorer at long last. The tall Scot was never a physical, bustling striker. Although he had something of a temper, he had skill in abundance and always had an eye for a spectacular goal (notably scoring a superb long-range effort in the team's excellent home win against a free-scoring Wigan side). Sometimes displaying an uninterested nonchalance on the pitch, he had the ability and the knack of suddenly coming to life to find a goal from nothing. He made 61 league appearances for the club, during which he found the net 25 times.

Darren Moore

Darren joined the Rovers in July 1995 from Torquay United for a then club record fee of £62,500. The size of the fee for the 21-year-old central defender may have initially raised a few eyebrows, but from the minute he made his debut in a Rovers shirt on the opening day of the 1995/96 season against Scarborough, it was clear he represented supreme value for money.

He quickly established himself as the rock which that Rovers side was built on and was superb in the middle of defence throughout a season in which Rovers should have at least made the play-offs. However, not for the first time, they missed out following a poor second half to the season. Darren never suffered with these inconsistencies himself, however, enjoying a great season on the pitch picking up the supporters' player of the year award.

Nicknamed 'Bruno' owing to his likeness to the heavyweight boxer, Darren's imposing physical stature must have been enough to put some strikers off their game before a ball was even kicked. Virtually unbeatable in the air, the big man was surprisingly sprightly across the turf too, regularly marauding forward with the ball at his feet. He was big, strong and quick, with good distribution skills, a towering powerful defender who always gave 100 per cent in a Rovers shirt. He quickly became a favourite with the fans, although it was clear he was always destined to play at a higher level.

His second season with the club went the same way as the first with Darren outstanding (once again winning the player of the year), but with the team's league position not matching his own personal endeavours and the club in deep financial trouble, it was clear he had to move on.

Bradford City won the race for his signature, with the £310,000 fee being set by a tribunal, but once again breaking the club's transfer record. He went on to become a key component at Valley Parade in the side which won promotion to the Premier League. Moore subsequently joined Portsmouth before heading to the Midlands where he enjoyed a hugely successful spell with West Brom and he again helped a team gain promotion to the top flight. He subsequently made a number of Premier League appearances as the club yo-yoed in and out of the division. He moved to Derby, who provided him with his fourth promotion to the country's elite division before joining Barnsley and then Burton Albion.

Darren is active within his role in the Christian charity Faith and Football, and in 2006 walked the Great Wall of China with friend and fellow professional footballer Linvoy Primus in order to raise money for children's causes.

He has enjoyed a superb career, playing in the Premier League and becoming a full international with Jamaica. His quality is shown by the amount of money clubs have paid out for his services, with around £2 million amassed in cumulative transfer fees during a career which has accrued over 500 league appearances. He made a total of 76 league appearances for the Rovers and scored 4 goals.

HAT-TRICKS

Number of hat-tricks (3+ goals) achieved by Rovers players:

Tom Keetley	15
Alick Jeffrey	6
Clarrie Jordan	4*
Peter Kitchen	3
Peter Doherty	3
Harold Keetley	3
Ian Duerden	3 (all in the Conference)

*Records show that Clarrie Jordan scored a further 4 hat-tricks for the Rovers during wartime competitions which would take his tally to 8!

This list confirms the notoriety of the club's most prolific ever forwards with Tom Keetley's total of 15 simply remarkable. The most recent scorers of more than one hat-trick in the Football League are Lee Turnbull and James Coppinger. Lee Turnbull managed a hat-trick in a notable 6–0 win at Hartlepool in 1989 and a 3–0 win at home against Aldershot in 1990. James Coppinger is the most recent player to notch more than one hat-trick for the club, with 3 goals against Norwich in September 2010 adding to his superb hat-trick against Southend in the League One play-off semi-final in 2008.

THE ONE THEY GAVE AWAY …

He fit the bill as the archetypal front man of the day. At 6ft 3in tall he was big and strong, good in the air and held the ball up well. This, allied with decent pace and the ability to run in behind defenders, meant Brian Deane had all the necessary qualities as a front man.

Undoubtedly talented, although still quite raw as he entered the first team, having been nurtured through the ranks, he performed well in a Rovers side which struggled. He eventually established himself as the team's talisman while still a teenager, ending the 1987/88 season as top scorer with a creditable 10 league goals.

With financial problems never far away, a move for one of the club's most saleable assets always looked on the cards and in the summer of 1988, Sheffield United acquired his services for a paltry £30,000. He went on to develop as his early promise suggested he might, scoring the goals which took Sheffield United to the top league in England. Indeed, he had the honour of scoring the first ever Premier League goal in 1992 when he made an early strike against Manchester United and went on to win 3 caps for England. His goals consistently caught the eye and he moved to Leeds for £2.9 million in 1993.

He continued to play at the highest level and moved briefly back to Bramall Lane in 1992 for £1.5 million before spells with Benfica, Middlesbrough, Leicester, West Ham, Leeds again and Sunderland. Over the course of his career he amassed transfer fees totalling in excess of £8.5 million and scored over 200 goals making him the jewel that the Rovers unearthed and then sold for relative peanuts.

ROVERS PLAYER OF THE SEASON

2010/11 Billy Sharp
2009/10 John Oster
2008/09 Matt Mills
2007/08 Richie Wellens
2006/07 Graeme Lee
2005/06 Sean Thornton
2004/05 Paul Green
2003/04 Michael McIndoe
2002/03 Paul Barnes
2001/02 Jamie Paterson
2000/01 Barry Miller
1999/2000 Dave Penney
1998/99 Lee Warren
1997/98 Lee Warren
1996/97 Darren Moore
1995/96 Darren Moore
1994/95 Russ Wilcox
1993/94 Russ Wilcox
1992/93 Eddie Gormley
1991/92 Eddie Gormley
1990/91 Colin Douglas

1989/90 Colin Douglas
1988/89 Jack Ashurst
1987/88 Ronnie Robinson
1986/87 Neil Redfearn
1985/86 Tony Brown
1984/85 Ian Snodin
1983/84 Colin Douglas
1982/83 Glynn Snodin
1981/82 Glynn Snodin
1980/81 Alan Little
1979/80 Alan Warboys
1978/79 Pat Lally
1977/78 Bobby Owen
1976/77 Ian Miller
1975/76 Ian Miller
1974/75 Peter Kitchen
1973/74 Mike Elwiss
1972/73 Archie Irvine
1971/72 Archie Irvine
1970/71 Brian Usher

CHEAP SEATS

When clubs move to new grounds, it is quite common for the seats from the old stadium to be sold off. When Stoke City left their Victoria Park home to start life at the Britannia Stadium, a number of the red plastic seats were sold off to fans. Always a club looking to save money, though, the Rovers bought a section of seating and installed the seats within the Main Stand at Belle Vue during the 1990s. Likewise, the Main Stand also contained seats bought from Sunderland when they left Roker Park!

CULT HEROES – JACK ASHURST

Jack joined in 1988 aged 34 for a reported fee of £15,000 from Leeds United. He brought with him vast experience and excellent organisational skills. A tough central defender, Ashurst could read the game extremely well and was never flustered, regardless of the situation in front of him.

He had a tremendous influence on the players around him and proved to be an excellent, strong leader on the pitch, qualities which were recognised as he was installed as club captain shortly after joining and was given the supporters' player of the year award in his first season.

Jack was released in May 1990, having turned down the offer of a new contract from the club in order to concentrate on business interests away from the game and joined non-league Bridlington Town. Five months later, however, Rovers boss Billy Bremner convinced him to re-sign as short-term cover for widespread injuries in the Rovers defensive personnel. This short-term agreement eventually lasted two years as Ashurst continued to turn in a number of reliable performances before he eventually left the club in August 1992, joining Rochdale on a non-contract basis.

Such was his impact, it was considered – in times of crisis, call Jack! He was an ever-reliable, excellent footballer who was a real fans' favourite and made a total of 149 appearances for the Rovers.

MANAGERIAL GREATS – PETER DOHERTY

April 1949 saw the club make one of the most important signings ever with the addition of Peter Doherty from Huddersfield Town for a fee of £8,000 as player-manager. Doherty was regarded as one of the finest players of his generation, a complete footballer with the ability to link defence to attack and score goals. He had won a League Championship with Manchester City and an FA Cup with Derby earlier in his career. 'Peter the Great' continued to have a huge impact on the field but off the field his impact was felt with even more resonance.

Doherty was vastly ahead of his time with his approach to coaching and training, criticising those who placed too much emphasis on hard running and strength work, instead advocating skills practice and decision-making exercises to develop his players. He had the vision to set up 'nursery clubs' to nurture and develop young players throughout South Yorkshire and the North-East before they would graduate to his first team. Doherty was also progressive in his attitude in developing an early loan system, allowing young players to sign for Midland League teams under the condition they would be allowed to rejoin the Rovers should their development reach the required level, with a clear dedication to securing the long-term future of the club by producing quality young players.

His impact on the team was immediate, winning 5 of his first 7 games in charge in a season which ultimately yielded the Third Division North title. The following season saw an impressive 11th place in Division Two with average gates over 22,000 and the club in a very healthy position with the promise of more.

Doherty was responsible for the signings and subsequent development of some very talented footballers in the likes of Eddie McMorran, Kit Lawlor, Chris Giles and Len Graham, all of whom earned senior caps for their country along with Barry Staton, Mike Connolly and Alick Jeffrey who represented England at under-23 and under-18 level. Indeed Doherty was said to have had a row with his friend Matt Busby when he won the race to sign a young Alick Jeffrey ahead of Manchester United, a feud which took many years to conclude. In addition, Doherty could take credit for the introduction of Harry Gregg who went on to become the most expensive goalkeeper in the world following his move from the Rovers to Manchester United for a then record £25,000.

For ten years Doherty shaped the fortune of the club securing a place in the second tier for most of them and reaching the fifth round of the FA Cup on four occasions during the club's most successful spell in its history.

Doherty also managed the Northern Ireland national side, guiding them to their first ever World Cup finals in 1958 where they produced their best-ever performance in reaching the quarter-finals.

Rovers struggled somewhat during the 1957/58 season, however, and the fans were amazed to hear of Doherty's resignation in January 1958 amid rumours of a falling out with some of the club's directors. The side managed only two further wins in the remainder of the season and were relegated twice in successive seasons – that was the hole left by such a popular and successful figure.

Record

	Played	Won	Lost	Drawn
Total	389	133	147	109

A LUCKY OWL

There is a story that Rovers used to have an owl that made a home high in the roof of the Main Stand at Belle Vue, and when Rovers played night games the owl was often seen around the ground. Legend has it that one evening the owl flew away and disappeared but that when the owl returned, the club's fortunes would change and the side would once again climb the Football League. John Ryan brought a stuffed owl to the club shortly after he successfully bought the Rovers and since then the club has never looked back, but this was surely merely a coincidence?

GREATEST GAMES

Doncaster Rovers 4–3 Manchester City, 7 October 1950
For all of the games throughout the history of Doncaster Rovers, the game against Manchester City on 7 October 1950 stills ranks as one of, if not the most exciting and dramatic matches ever. Both sides were new to the Second Division, albeit their journeys coming from opposite directions. Rovers had just achieved promotion from the Third Division while City had come down from the First. Rovers had made a decent start to life at a higher level and had only lost 2 of the first 10 games, recording 3 wins along the way. City were flying, however, and were still unbeaten while sitting on the very top of the division, as they visited Doncaster for the first time in the league for nearly 50 years.

The Lancashire side got the perfect start with Syd Bycroft's mistimed header falling perfectly for Smith who had time to control the ball before placing it past Hardwick in the Rovers goal to give the visitors the lead. City poured forward in numbers, sensing a second goal, and just after the half hour it duly arrived courtesy of another neat finish from City forward Smith. Things went from bad to worse when, with 3 minutes left to play before half time, a long ball into the Rovers' box found Westcott whose knock-down fell to Smith once more, who poked home to complete a first-half hat-trick.

City had been outstanding throughout the first half, showing exactly why they had enjoyed such a great start to the season. By contrast Rovers had been totally anonymous in a game where they hadn't even had a chance to get hold of the ball and play. With the Rovers defence looking utterly shell-shocked there seemed no way back for the home side; City looked in a different league, and more goals appeared likely to follow.

The Rovers fans knew that the team had to start well if they were to have any chance of salvaging something from the second half, and fortunately that's just what they did. The players emerged for the second half with the bit between their teeth and, within 5 minutes of the game restarting, Calverly found some room out on the flank and was able to fire a cross into the box towards Harrison. The Rovers centre-forward got to the ball first and directed the ball past City keeper Bert Trautmann to record his fourth goal of the season.

Barely 2 minutes later, Irishman Kit Lawlor found some space in sight of the City goal with the ball at his feet and noticed Trautmann had strayed slightly off his line. Lawlor measured the most delicate of lobs over the goalkeeper into the net. Suddenly, with the score at 3–2, Rovers were in the game again.

There was scarcely chance to catch your breath as just moments later, Rovers' Lowes fired a shot goalwards only for City defender Rigby to keep the ball out with his hand. Up stepped Rovers player-manager Peter Doherty, playing against his former club with whom he had become a legend in winning the League Championship some 13 years earlier, who coolly dispatched the spot-kick for his fifth goal of the campaign. Over 30,000 spectators held their breath in anticipation of what was to follow in this incredible game.

Rovers flooded forward and Doherty set off towards the heart of the City defence, jinking in and out of City defenders before letting fly with a drive that flashed past Trautmann from fully 25 yards; incredibly, within 2 minutes of the equaliser, Rovers were ahead 4–3. Manchester City had been caught cold in a scintillating period of football from the home side that saw 4 goals scored inside a 10-minute spell. Peter Doherty's drive proved the final, decisive goal of an amazing game which handed Rovers the most unlikely of victories and probably the greatest comeback in the club's history.

Without question, the bumper attendance of 32,937 had certainly got value for money, especially those who were watching from the Rossington end of Belle Vue, as all 7 goals were scored at that end!

BALDERSTONE'S BUSY DAY

On 15 September 1975, Rovers midfielder Chris Balderstone made history by becoming the first man to play first-class cricket and League football in the same day! A talented cricketer playing with Leicestershire, Balderstone was part of a team pushing towards the County Championship and engaged in a crucial match with Derbyshire at Chesterfield. He spent the day in the field before being called upon with the bat, ending the day on 51 not out, and with the game in the balance. At stumps he made the dash to South Yorkshire, arriving at Belle Vue still in his whites, with enough time only for a cup of tea and a quick change into his Rovers shirt, before playing his part in a 1–1 draw with Brentford.

The following day, Balderstone returned to Chesterfield where he completed a hugely impressive century before taking 3 second-innings wickets which helped Leicestershire claim their first ever County Championship trophy. Remarkably, Balderstone made over 500 Football League appearances and notched up 390 first-class cricket matches, scoring over 19,000 runs at an average over 34 and also took 310 wickets at an average of 26. Such was his talent that he actually played in two Test matches for England in 1976 against the hugely impressive West Indies side, during the kind of fairytale career most of us could only dream of.

ROVERS GREATS – 2000s

Paul Heffernan
Paul joined the Rovers during the summer of 2005 with manager Dave Penney breaking the club's transfer record by spending £125,000 to secure his services. He had started out with Notts County where his impressive goalscoring record led to a move to Bristol City for £150,000. He found opportunities at Ashton Gate limited, however, leading to his move to South Yorkshire.

An out-and-out striker, Heffernan's game developed throughout his stay with the Rovers and, already an excellent finisher and goalscorer, he added an increased work ethic and ability to hold the ball up and bring others into play, to his game. Surprisingly quick, he displayed a habit of finding space in the box and regularly delivered important goals for the club. Often going a few games without a goal, he'd burst into life and find a goalscoring run of form.

He played a big part in Rovers' excellent Carling Cup run in 2005, notably scoring with a super finish against Aston Villa. Indeed it was cup competitions where Heffernan arguably found most success for Doncaster and made a huge contribution to the victory in the Johnstone's Paint Trophy in 2007. Heffernan scored 2 goals in each of the two legs of the semi-final win against Crewe, including a nerve-wracking penalty which proved crucial and had to be retaken. Heffernan proved his goalscoring instincts by smashing the retake home in much the same fashion as he had the first.

He was also instrumental in the final, recovering from injury in time for the game. He set up Jonathon Forte's early opener before running through to fire home a superb left-footed drive himself as Rovers raced into an early 2-goal lead.

Heffernan, sadly, missed the League One play-off final at Wembley through suspension, having been sent off in the semi-final. However he was to play a pivotal role in the club's survival in the Championship the following year. His brace at Nottingham Forest on Boxing Day helped Rovers to a 4–2 win that set the club on the run which lifted them off the foot of the table and to safety, with Heffernan scoring 10 league goals in the second half of the season, finishing as the club's top scorer once again.

His goals guaranteed him as a fans' favourite and when he left for Sheffield Wednesday in the summer of 2010 after five years with the Rovers, it was with everyone's best wishes. Paul played 127 league games for the club, scoring 36 times, but made a total of 160 appearances, scoring 54 times.

Paul Green

Green joined the club as a teenager during the Rovers' time in the Conference, making his debut on 19 March 2002 against Northwich. He made his full debut three days later, scoring in a 5–2 win against Hayes at Belle Vue.

He went on to become a regular in midfield, forming a partnership with the more defensively minded Ricky Ravenhill. Paul was encouraged to push forward and get into the opponents' box. He was the archetypal, all-action, box-to-box midfielder, covering every blade of grass on the pitch throughout 90 minutes. Full of running and a neat passer with an eye for goal, he became a key player as the side made the Conference play-offs and was identified as one of the key players going into the final. He did not disappoint, producing a superb display, winning man of the match and scoring the Rovers' first goal as they won promotion back to the Football League.

He remained a pivotal figure in the side from then on, his drive and his goals from midfield proving to be one of the reasons Rovers won the Third Division championship the following year. He won the Johnstone's Paint Trophy with the club in 2007 and was again a major force in the team, particularly during the second half of the 2007/08 season as Rovers went into the final game needing a victory at Cheltenham to gain promotion to the Championship. Things didn't go Rovers' way that afternoon, despite Paul bursting into the area to notch a trademark goal, but he went on to play an important part in the biggest day in the club's history – winning the play-off final at Wembley.

He caused a real shock among the supporters when he moved to Derby County that summer, declining to sign a new contract with Rovers who could not match Derby's offer. He did, however, receive a standing ovation from the Rovers supporters as he made his Derby debut against Doncaster in August 2008.

He has been a great success in a Derby side that have largely struggled with life in the Championship, and Paul won a call-up to the Republic of Ireland squad in 2010, scoring in his second appearance in a 3–0 win over Algeria.

Paul was always a popular figure with Rovers supporters, who watched him grow up in the centre of midfield. He was the only member of the squad who made the journey from the Conference to the Championship having won three promotions with the club and for the significant part he played, he will always be held in high regard. He made 198 league appearances and scored 25 goals and in total made 234 appearances and scored 27 times following the club's promotion back into League football.

Michael McIndoe

Michael McIndoe joined Rovers in the summer of 2003 as the club were preparing for life back in the Football League. He had also spent the previous year in the Conference, playing a starring role in winning the championship with Yeovil, so Rovers manager Dave Penney had seen at first-hand what he was getting as the club paid out £50,000 for the Scottish winger.

McIndoe was an instant success, playing a hugely important role in the team that went on the win the Third Division that year, and was selected for the PFA Division Three team of the year. He finished second in the club's goalscoring chart for the season – from midfield – a feat which he replicated the following season in League One.

His talents were placed in the national spotlight during the club's Carling Cup run in 2005, during which he was the side's talisman, scoring crucial goals against Premier League giants Manchester City, Aston Villa and Arsenal on Rovers' unlikely run to the quarter-finals. McIndoe was included in the Scotland 'B' squad and was once again selected in the divisional team of the year; such was the impact he had at Belle Vue.

He ultimately left the club because of his desire to play at a higher level, going on loan to Derby County before then signing for then newly promoted Barnsley in the Championship for a fee reported to be £125,000. Subsequent moves to Wolves, Bristol City and Coventry City followed, each for a sizable fee.

McIndoe was a superb goalscoring winger during his time at Belle Vue, his pace and natural ability made him a handful for any defence and he always seemed to deliver a quality end product. He was one of those players who could produce something out of nothing and turn a game in the blink of an eye, as he did on so many occasions. The huge impact he had on the team throughout his stay with the club meant he was always a favourite with the fans. He was never shy of doing the hard work, tracking back when required and working hard for the team, attributes which went a long way to ensuring the status he gained within the club.

He made 122 league appearances for the Rovers, scoring 28 goals and in total he turned out 142 times for the club, managing 35 goals.

THEY SAID IT

'We're all enjoying being up there and it's a feeling we don't want to lose. We have got off to an excellent start and the players have set their own high standards. It is up to them to keep it going.'

Billy Bremner at the start of the 1990/91 season in the middle of Rovers wining the first 5 games of the season. A couple of weeks later and the side couldn't keep it going, losing 4 games in a row

'If there is a big noise and a great atmosphere it definitely makes a difference and we need the fans to get behind us like never before.'

Dave Penney recognises the importance of a hostile Belle Vue ahead of the play-off semi-final with Chester in 2003

'Football is a funny business, anything can happen.'

Peter Doherty, reported following his side's sensational comeback against Manchester City to win 4–3 in 1950

DISASTERS ...

November 1998 saw the club play its first ever tie in the FA Trophy following its relegation to the Conference. The draw was seemingly kind to the Rovers and provided a home tie with local minnows Frickley Athletic. Frickley were struggling in the Unibond Premier and surely most of the impressive crowd of over 2,000 that day expected to see nothing other than a comfortable home win. ...

The visitors had other ideas and a spirited display left Rovers red-faced and beaten 2–0 in a result which is probably one of the worst in the club's history.

CULT HEROES – BARRY MILLER

The physical, tough-tackling central defender made his Rovers debut at Boston in a Conference game during 2000 and almost instantly cemented himself as a huge favourite among the Rovers fans. Good in the air and never shy of a physical confrontation, Barry was able to read the game well and always appeared composed and thoughtful on the ball.

Loved by the fans on the 'Pop Side' at Belle Vue, he was always a popular figure on the terraces and was nicknamed 'Covered in Monkeys' due to his immovable and steadfast qualities making him 'like a rock' (you can't question logic like that). He arguably enjoyed his most acclaimed moment in a Rovers shirt in 2001 when late on in a win at Northwich, Barry decided he'd simply had enough of opposing forward Jimmy Quinn, whose distinguished career cut no ice with Barry who landed a punch on the former Northern Ireland international. Sadly, the referee was the only person in the ground who failed to enjoy the moment and gave Barry his marching orders.

An excellent and committed pro as well as a likeable character, Barry remains a cult figure having made a total of 69 league appearances and scored twice during his time at Belle Vue.

ROVERS FOREIGN XI

Historically the Rovers have never been the most fashionable or cosmopolitan of clubs, but in the modern era of foreign imports, a look back over past players reveals that the Rovers could field a team of foreigners who have all had the honour of wearing the famous red and white of Doncaster. Not all made contributions which will live long in the memory and they all had differing degrees of success.

Jan Budtz
(Denmark)

Shelton Martis   Jos Van Nieuwstadt
(Holland)   (Holland)
Ignacio Ybarra   Dave Mulligan
(Spain)   (New Zealand)

Quinton Fortune   Nicolas Priet
(South Africa)   (France)
Dino Maamria
(Tunisia)

Gunnar Torfason   Michele Di Piedi
(Iceland)   (Italy)
Guy Ipoua
(Cameroon)

DISASTERS ...

Rovers travelled to Spotland in September 1996 looking for a victory against a Rochdale side still without a first league win of the season. Things started well for the visitors as Rochdale had central defender Keith Hill sent off after only 14 minutes – and he was followed by striker Mark Leonard as Rochdale ended the first half with 9 men!

Rovers made their two-man advantage pay in the second half, working the ball around well, comfortably retaining possession before their efforts were rewarded by winger Ian Clark's neat finish on 69 minutes, surely ensuring Rovers would stroll to victory. . . .

However, home captain John Deary equalised and in the final 8 minutes Dave Thompson inexplicably found acres of room to pull the ball back for Andy Gouck to slip a winner past keeper Dean Williams. The away side, having played the entire second half of the game with two extra men, contrived to snatch defeat from the jaws of victory!

HAT-TRICKS

The Rovers' first ever Football League hat-trick was scored by full-back Ike Marsh. He netted 3 times as Rovers beat Chesterfield 4–1 at home in January 1902.

The first ever hat-trick by a Rovers player came on 17 October 1891 in a match against Wednesbury Old Athletic when centre-forward Charles Waddington helped himself to three goals in a 4–1 win.

There have only been three occasions in the club's history when a Rovers player has scored a hat-trick and the side have not managed to win the game. The first was in December 1950 when Rovers were held to a 4–4 draw at home to Leeds United despite a hat-trick from Peter Doherty. 4–4 was also the final score on 29 September 1956 when Alick Jeffrey notched a treble in a league game at Bury. On 15 November 1966 Rovers lost an incredible game at home to Mansfield 6–4 despite Trevor Ogden keeping the match ball!

The highest number of goals ever scored by an individual Rovers player in a single game stands at an incredible tally of 6. Legendary forward Tom Keetley scored 6 of Rovers' 7 goals on 16 February 1929 during an amazing afternoon which saw a total of 11 goals in the game, as Rovers beat Ashington 7–4 away from home.

Incidentally, a Rovers player has managed 5 goals in a game on only one occasion – 6 years to the day following Keetley's record 6 goals, Albert Turner managed 5 for the Rovers as they beat New Brighton in a slightly more one-sided game, 7–1.

TOP CUP RUNS

League Cup 2005/06
The Carling Cup run in 2005 will live long in the memory of all Rovers fans. Those cold, uncomfortably cramped nights epitomised all that was great about Belle Vue and gave the Rovers their last 'big nights' at the ground.

The atmospheres at the games against Premier League Manchester City, Aston Villa and Arsenal provided a perfect backdrop for underdog triumphs, with the home fans packed inside, lining the touchlines and almost on top of the players. The noise echoed around the ageing wooden seats in the Main Stand on the crispest of cold Yorkshire evenings, creating a real cauldron of noise and intimidation as only Belle Vue could.

Happily, the players did not disappoint and having won away at Wrexham in the first round, Rovers lined up against Manchester City. The game was a close, evenly fought contest which bubbled over into extra time, where England striker Darius Vassell looked to have won the game for City with a neatly converted penalty. Things got worse as Rovers keeper Andy Warrington suffered a broken leg, but late on striker Paul Heffernan went down in the area and Michael McIndoe converted to send the tie to penalties. Some crucial saves from replacement keeper Jan Budtz sent Rovers through on a memorable night.

The third round saw Rovers beat Gillingham 2–0 thanks to two late Paul Heffernan goals which brought Aston Villa to town. Once again Belle Vue was rocking as Rovers produced some sparkling football to comprehensively beat a full-strength Villa team, full of internationals, assembled for tens of millions of pounds. McIndoe put the Rovers ahead from the spot and Doncaster went on to simply overwhelm their Premiership opponents with a football lesson. Heffernan added a second with a crisp finish from the edge of the box before Sean Thornton added a superb long-range third as Rovers waltzed into the quarter-finals.

Arsène Wenger's Arsenal team boasted a World Cup winner among a host of big names, but they too found Belle Vue an uninviting prospect. Rovers once again flew out of the blocks as McIndoe squeezed an early effort home to put the home side 1–0 up. Rovers matched their illustrious visitors throughout but Arsenal equalised just past the hour and again extra time was needed. Paul Green bundled Rovers ahead and with seconds remaining – it looked as though the unthinkable would happen. However, the

Gunners galloped downfield and Gilberto swept home an equaliser. It was a cruel blow and one which Rovers never recovered from, losing in the shoot-out. The home side rightly won the plaudits for another splendid footballing display, a performance which was against an excellent Arsenal team that would make it to the Champions League final a few months later, but it was of little consolation in the chill of that December night.

It still remained one of the greatest cup runs in the history of the club, summed up by the chants of 'we're very proud of you' which rang round Belle Vue's creaking terraces.

First Round, 23 August 2005
Wrexham   0–1   Doncaster Rovers
                                   Hughes
Rovers: Warrington, McGuire, Ryan, Fenton, Foster, Mulligan, Coppinger, Ravenhill, Fortune-West, Guy, McIndoe. Subs: Hughes for Ravenhill (59), Offiong for Coppinger (71), Heffernan, McDaid, Richardson.
Attendance: 2,177

Second Round, 21 September 2005
Doncaster Rovers   1–1   Manchester City
                                   (aet, 0–0 after 90 mins)
McIndoe (pen)
Rovers won 3–0 on penalties.
Rovers: Warrington, McGuire, McDaid, S. Roberts, Albrighton, Green, Coppinger, Predic, Fortune-West, Guy, McIndoe. Subs: Ravenhill for Predic (52), Heffernan for Guy (81), Budtz for Warrington (105), N. Roberts, Mulligan.
Pens: McIndoe scored 1–0, Vassell missed 1–0, Coppinger scored 2–0, Sibierski saved 2–0, Heffernan scored 3–0, Dunne saved 3–0.
Attendance: 8,228

Third Round, 25 October 2005

Doncaster Rovers   2–0   Gillingham
Heffernan (2)
Rovers: Budtz, Marples, McDaid, S. Roberts, Albrighton,
Ravenhill, Coppinger, Green, N. Roberts, Guy, McIndoe.
Subs: Thornton for Ravenhill (69), Heffernan for
N. Roberts (73) Fortune-West for Guy (90), Fenton,
Richardson.
Attendance: 6,874

Fourth Round, 29 November 2005

Doncaster Rovers   3–0   Aston Villa
McIndoe (pen)
Heffernan
Thornton
Rovers: Seremet, Fenton, Mulligan, S. Roberts, Foster,
Ravenhill, Coppinger, Thornton, Heffernan, Guy,
McIndoe. Subs: Green for Guy (87), N. Roberts, Fortune-
West, Oji, Budtz.
Attendance: 10,590

Quarter-Final, 21 Decemeber2005

Doncaster Rovers   2–2   Arsenal (aet, 1–1 after 90 mins)
McIndoe
Green
Arsenal won 3–1 on penalties
Rovers: Budtz, Fenton, S. Roberts, Foster, McDaid,
Coppinger, Thornton, Ravenhill, McIndoe, Heffernan,
Guy. Subs: Green for Thornton (85), N. Roberts for
Coppinger, Oji for Guy (115), Nielsen, Fortune-West.
Attendance: 10,006

DISASTERS ...

The 1989/90 season had been a difficult one for the Rovers, spending most of it at the wrong end of the table, but as the season came to a close, Rovers looked like giving their long-suffering supporters a break. On 21 April 1990 Rovers entertained Halifax at Belle Vue and off the back of a couple of decent results, raced into a 3–0 lead. Goals from Turnbull, Muir and Grayson put Rovers in total control inside half an hour and when the players came out for the second half, the majority of Rovers fans were wondering how many we would get.

What followed still torments me, bringing me to a cold sweat in the middle of dark nights. I recall my Dad pointed out that Rovers keeper Mark Samways 'looked a bit dazed' following a knock on the head, but thinking nothing more of it, I settled in for the second half goal-fest Rovers would surely deliver. At the end of 90 minutes, 'Sammy' wasn't the only one whose head was spinning. Rovers somehow managed to never really lose their superiority in the game, but somehow contrived to concede 4 second-half goals and the 2,232 people who watched that game were left scratching their heads. It was a result that only the Rovers team of that time could have managed!

FOUR-GOAL HAULS

Thirteen games in the club's history have seen a single player score 4 goals in a game for the Rovers (excluding the war years). Tom Keetley contributed 5 of those occasions on his own, with the others to achieve this milestone in the Football League being Ronnie Dodd, Peter Clark, Alfie Hale and Alick Jeffrey. Mick Killourhy and Glen Kirkwood managed 4 in FA Cup ties, and forwards Chester and Vail managed the feat in the Midland League around the turn of the twentieth century.

SHARP'S RECORD

Rovers' visit to the Walkers Stadium for a Championship game in December 2010 turned out to be a record-breaker! Billy Sharp scored early to give Rovers the lead, with the goal being the Rovers striker's 100th of his career and also the 300th goal that the Rovers had managed under manager Sean O'Driscoll. The only black spot on the day was the rest of the afternoon, as Rovers went on to lose the match 5–1!

ATTENDANCE INCREASE

The club's average attendance rose by an amazing 97.1 per cent in 1998/99, despite having been relegated from the Football League the previous season. Supporters who had stayed away in their droves as a result of Ken Richardson's ownership of the club, returned to celebrate to club's revival under John Ryan. Despite playing in the Conference, the club averaged 3,380 as opposed to 1,715 during the club's worst ever season.

GREATEST GAMES

Rovers 5–4 Dover, 19 December 1998

December 1998 saw the club bottom of the Football League with everyone involved with the club simply delighted to be there. Months earlier the town had mourned the death of a once proud and dignified football club which had since been dramatically brought back to life. However, they were feeling the pressure having not won in the league for a month and had only notched up 3 wins all season.

Dover set about the home side right from the off, enjoying too much space early on, a mistake which would harm Rovers, badly. As early as the 4th minute, the visitors took the lead when big striker Joff Vansittart (who hadn't scored in the league for four months) headed home from close range. Worse was to follow as Vansittart exposed the Rovers defence twice more with neat headers from well-worked set pieces, and the big striker claimed a hat-trick after only 27 minutes.

The terraces were stunned into a silent disbelief with the home side seemingly dead and buried at 3–0 down inside half an hour. Just as the half came to a close, Rovers found a lifeline from a set piece of their own. Capitalising on some confusion in the penalty box, Glenn Kirkwood nipped in to poke home a scruffy goal to scrape into the interval 3–1 down.

The Rovers management must have had their say at half time, as the side emerged galvanized by the challenge in front of them; superbly led by skipper Dave Penney the Rovers midfield began to grab the game by the scruff of the neck. Penney, who had acquired a reputation for scoring spectacular goals, picked up a loose ball in the centre of the park. The crowd, pleading with him to 'hit it!', watched as the Rovers skipper unleashed a sweetly struck drive from all of 25 yards which flashed into the corner of the net.

Visibly driven on by Penney in midfield, Ian Duerden tried to slip Kirkwood through but the ball ran loose on the edge of the penalty area, straight into the path of the onrushing Dino Maamria, who crashed a shot into the bottom right-hand corner and the teams were amazingly back square at 3–3.

Surely now Rovers would press home the advantage and find a winner? Once again, however, Dover had other ideas and out of nothing Hynes beat Woods with a neatly placed shot to put Dover back in front at 4–3 with only 11 minutes left.

Again Belle Vue fell silent but again it was Penney who dragged the team forward. He tossed the ball high into the box and, under pressure from Duerden and Maamria; Dover defender Buddon could only divert the ball into his own net. Belle Vue erupted once more, 9 minutes left and the game really was anyone's at 4–4.

Rovers managed to carve out one final throw of the dice late on. Again the ball was played into the feet of the impressive Duerden and the striker spun off his marker before wrong-footing the defence with a neat backheel into the path of Kirkwood who hammered home a glorious winner. It was a goal worthy of deciding such an epic blockbuster of a game, one of the most incredible and astonishing games in the club's history.

THEY SAID IT

'It is a big wrench physically and emotionally. I had a sleepless night but when I woke up with a clear head I decided it was the right move.'

Sean O'Driscoll understandably having some doubts when contemplating swapping life on the South Coast for South Yorkshire

'Around the October time I think we won 11 out of 13. Everyone was expecting us to fall away. I think we caught everyone on the hop, they didn't know what we were all about.'

Dave Penney on the 2003/04 season, which his side began as favourites for relegation but proved everyone wrong and raced to a record points total and the Third Division title

DISASTERS ...

On Tuesday 10 December 2002, Rovers travelled to Gresty Road for what looked like a tough encounter with a talented Crewe Alexandra team for an LDV Vans Northern quarter-final tie. Going well in the Conference, Rovers fielded a strong team with the prize of a Wembley final now just a few games away. This tricky tie was even tougher by half time as Crewe led 3–0, and any chance of climbing the mountain was soon gone with Crewe never letting up. Inspired by a hat-trick from future England striker Dean Ashton, Alexandra eventually ended 8–0 winners!

TOP LEAGUE GOALSCORERS

Tom Keetley	180 goals
Alick Jeffrey	127 goals
Bert Tindall	125 goals
Peter Kitchen	89 goals
Brendan O'Callaghan	65 goals

TOP GOALSCORERS, 50+

(Senior competitions only, excludes war leagues)

Tom Keetley	186 goals
Alick Jeffrey	139 goals
Bert Tindall	134 goals
Peter Kitchen	105 goals
Brendan O'Callaghan	77 goals
Colin Booth	62 goals
Colin Douglas	62 goals
Glynn Snodin	62 goals
Peter Doherty	59 goals
Paul Todd	56 goals
Stan Burton	54 goals
Paul Heffernan	54 goals
Bert Turner	53 goals
Ray Harrison	50 goals
Clarrie Jordan	50 goals

20 GOALS A SEASON SCORERS

20 goals in a season is the benchmark of all top strikers and so it is unsurprising that the names of some genuine Rovers legends make up the bulk of this list, with the amazing goalscoring talents of Tom Keetley featuring most heavily. Rovers' record goalscorer reached the magic number of 20 goals for an amazing 6 consecutive seasons for the club, a feat unlikely to ever be matched.

Peter Kitchen, another great Rovers goal-getter, reached the milestone on three consecutive seasons during the 1970s with the greatest of them all, Alick Jeffrey, notching more than 20 twice in the 1960s. Here is the full list, every name a true goalscorer, without exception.

Key: ML – Midland League, WL – War League, WLC –
War League Cups, FL – Football League, Conf – Football
Conference (includes play-off rounds), FA – FA Cup,
LC – League Cup, FT – Football League Trophy, W –
Wharncliffe League (this was to supplement the Midland
League during the First World War)

1898/99	Gladwin	20 Goals (13 ML, 7 FA)
1900/01	Vail	23 Goals (21 ML, 2 FA)
1900/01	Goodson	22 Goals (19 ML, 3 FA)
1908/09	Jex	20 Goals (20 ML)
1910/11	Jex	28 Goals (23 ML, 5 FA)
1910/11	Green	25 Goals (23 ML, 2 FA)
1915/16	Brown	22 Goals (15 ML, 7 W)
1922/23	Boardman	27 Goals (25 ML, 2 FA)
1923/24	T. Keetley	21 Goals (21 FL)
1924/25	T. Keetley	27 Goals (23 FL, 4 FA)
1925/26	T. Keetley	24 Goals (24 FL)
1926/27	T. Keetley	37 Goals (36 FL, 1 FA)
1927/28	T. Keetley	36 Goals (36 FL)
1928/29	T. Keetley	41 Goals (40 FL, 1 FA)
1932/33	Waterston	24 Goals (24 FL)
1933/34	Dodd	24 Goals (24 FL)
1934/35	Turner	25 Goals (25 FL)
1934/35	Baines	21 Goals (21 FL)
1937/38	Perry	24 Goals (24 FL)
1940/41	Bodle	23 Goals (23 WL)
1944/45	Bodle	27 Goals (14 WL, 13 WLC)
1944/45	Jordan	27 Goals (13 WL, 14 WLC)
1946/47	Jordan	44 Goals (42 FL, 2 FA)
1946/47	Todd	26 Goals (23 FL, 3 FA)
1949/50	Doherty	30 Goals (27 FL, 3 FA)
1959/60	Fernie	21 Goals (19 FL, 2 FA)
1962/63	Booth	38 Goals (34 FL, 2 FA, 2 LC)
1963/64	Booth	24 Goals (FL 23, FA 1)

1963/64	Hale	21 Goals (20 FL, 1 FA)
1964/65	Jeffrey	39 Goals (36 FL, 2 FA, 1 LC)
1965/66	Jeffrey	22 Goals (22 FL)
1965/66	Sheffield	28 Goals (28 FL)
1974/75	Kitchen	24 Goals (21 FL, 2 FA, 1 LC)
1975/76	Kitchen	24 Goals (22 FL, 2 LC)
1975/76	O'Callaghan	28 Goals (22 FL, 6 LC)
1976/77	Kitchen	27 Goals (23 FL, 3 FA, 1 LC)
1996/97	Cramb	21 Goals (18 FL, 1 FA, 1 LC, 1 FT)
2002/03	Barnes	28 Goals (26 Conf, 2 FA)
2003/04	Blundell	20 Goals (18 FL, 2 LC)
2006/07	Heffernan	21 Goals (11 FL, 1 FA, 9 FT)

CULT HEROES – EDDIE GORMLEY

Joining the club on a free transfer in July 1990 from Tottenham Hotspur, the Irish midfielder went on to make 128 appearances and score 17 goals during three years in South Yorkshire. Eddie was an all-action, box-to-box midfielder with the ability to drag his team back into a game. He won the player of the year award in 1992 and 1993 and was affectionately known as 'Steady Eddie' as the fans pleaded with him to go steady in the middle of the park. A tireless runner with a creative flair and eye for goal from long range, he was a big hit with the fans until his departure, deciding to play in his native Ireland, where he enjoyed a suitably successful career.

A WINLESS STREAK

During the 1997/98 season the Rovers took 21 matches before registering a league win. It wasn't until December 1997 that the side managed to accrue their first 3 points thanks to a 2–1 home victory over Chester City.

MORE RECORDS BROKEN

Rovers beat Middlesbrough 2–1 at the Keepmoat in December 2010 and in doing so recorded the club's 200th victory in the second tier. James Hayter's header was the Rovers' opening goal that evening and was also the 500th the club have managed at that level.

DISASTERS ...

February 2011 saw Rovers in crisis having slipped away from the play-off places following a dreadful run of form following the turn of the year as the season was derailed by a host of crippling injuries to a squad which lacked depth given the club's limited resources. Things got worse for the side, desperately short on confidence, as they prepared to entertain Ipswich at the Keepmoat – Rovers lost record signing Billy Sharp and skipper Brian Stock on the morning of the game to injury. Their names were added to an injury list which numbered in double figures and Rovers boss Sean O'Driscoll, now without a single available striker, was forced to cobble together a makeshift XI. Often however, when a side's back is so firmly up against the wall as this, the players produce a surprise reaction and pull something out of the most improbable hat and turn in the kind of spirited display which makes a mockery of such adverse a terrain.

Actually, not this time.

Sam Hird headed into his own net midway through the first half with the calamity setting the tone for the rest of the game. 3–0 down at half time, Rovers limped to a 6–0 defeat, the worst in the league at home, ever!

SINGING FOR THE CUP

In March 2007, one of Doncaster's favourite sons, 1980s rock icon John Parr, released 'Walking out of the Darkness' – a tribute to Doncaster Rovers' achievement in reaching the final of the Johnstone's Paint Football League Trophy final, and the club's first ever 'cup final song' was born. The week prior to the final saw Parr perform a special version of the single to hoards of fans, live in the town, as cup final fever started to take hold. The single was only available from the Doncaster branch of HMV and while it was also available online, somehow it surprisingly didn't quite make it to number 1 in the UK charts. In the end though, this disappointment was balanced out by a thrilling victory in the final.

KIT DISASTERS

The 1992/93 season Rovers struggled to avoid relegation in a battle which lasted the entire season, but was more notable as it saw the players proudly sporting what is surely the club's worst ever strip. The home shirt looked like a red and white hooped jersey which had been pumped full of 20,000 volts. The red hoops bounced up and down so violently that they looked like they were the reading of a heart monitor attached to Johnny Vegas running a marathon!

As if this wasn't bad enough, the away shirt provided no respite whatsoever. A crisp plain white shite was covered in what can only be described as red and green tentacles which draped themselves horrifically over the wearer's right shoulder.

CONFERENCE YEARS

The five long years spent in the Conference may be light years away from where the club finds itself now, but they undoubtedly played a huge part in laying the foundations that the more recent successes are built on. It is still remembered as a time when Rovers were the biggest fish in what was, granted, only a small pond, with great fondness by many. For the record, the Rovers' complete record during the Conference years is:

Season	Pld	W	D	L	F	A	Pts	Final Pos
1998/99	42	12	12	18	51	55	48	16th
1999/2000	42	15	9	18	46	48	54	12th
2000/01	42	15	13	14	47	43	58	9th
2001/02	42	18	13	11	68	46	67	4th
2002/03	42	22	12	8	73	47	78	3rd
Total	210	82	59	69	285	239	305	

DISASTERS ...

1997 saw the Rovers drawn against First Division Nottingham Forest in the first round of the League Cup. Forest had just been relegated from the Premier League and still had a first team littered with familiar names. At the time, the set up at the City Ground was light years ahead of the Rovers but with the first leg at Belle Vue, even I dared to dream of an upset. I made an agreement with my Dad that if we kept within 5 goals of Forest that he'd buy my ticket for the return leg in Nottingham. The first game kicked off and Rovers went close to a breakthrough early on, so I settled back in my seat confident that my wager was safe and even started to dream of a giant killing.

The following 89 minutes proved my Dad knew a thing or two and Forest ran riot, thumping the Rovers 8–0!

TOP FLIGHT XI

There are a number of players in recent times who have enjoyed spells with the Rovers and gone on to play for clubs in the top level of English football. The XI listed below did just that and would have made quite a team!

1. Harry Gregg
2. Ian Snodin
3. Rufus Brevett
4. Darren Moore
5. Chris Swailes
6. Terry Curran
7. Jamie Lawrence
8. Neil Redfearn
9. Brian Deane
10. Brendan O'Callaghan
11. Glynn Snodin

THE YORKSHIRE ELECTRICITY CUP

The 1995/96 season opened with a league match against Scarborough at Belle Vue, in a game which was notable by the silverware on offer. As well as the 3 valuable league points, the match was also billed as the 'Yorkshire Electricity Cup Final'. Happily the Rovers won this most unique of double-headers thanks to a second-half Sean Parrish goal and were subsequently presented with the cup after the match (it proved to be the only thing in the trophy cabinet for some time afterwards).

THE BOY DONE GOOD

Armthorpe-born forward Kevin Keegan was once famously rejected by the Rovers. As a youth on trial with the club, legend has it that he was turned away for being 'too small'. Whoever made that decision must have never lived it down as Keegan went on to win four league titles at home and abroad, an FA Cup, a League Cup and a European Cup as well as twice winning the Ballon d'Or (European footballer of the year) and earning more than 60 caps for England, before being inducted into the English Football Hall of Fame in 2002.

A similar misjudgment was evident in 1977 when Rovers took young forward Tony Woodcock on loan from Nottingham Forest with a view to a permanent move. Woodcock made an impression while with the Rovers, but the management chose to haggle with Forest over the small fee involved in making the deal permanent. Forest pulled out and Woodcock remained at the City Ground where he went on to win the league title, the League Cup, the Charity Shield, the European Cup, the European Super Cup and was crowned PFA Young Player of the Year. He also went on to play 42 times for England!

GEORGE RAYNOR

In the summer of 1967, Rovers installed former Coventry City boss George Raynor as manager. Raynor lasted little over a year as his team, which was never short of goals, struggled for wins away from Belle Vue. Raynor was consigned to history as a name on a long list of Rovers managers, but the story of his career prior to his return to South Yorkshire is nothing short of remarkable and offers clear evidence that the club may have had one of the game's best ever coaches at the helm. Indeed, his legacy has never received the recognition he deserved.

A Barnsley-born lad, he made a career from football as something of a journeyman in the lower leagues until the Second World War when he was working as a training instructor in Baghdad. Here he constructed the basis of an Iraq national side before returning to England. His overseas achievements had not gone unnoticed and he was recommended to the Swedish FA as they looked for a national coach in 1946.

Raynor led his side back to Britain for the 1948 Olympic Games, where quite amazingly and against all the odds, they won the gold medal beating a strong Yugoslavia in the final, and eclipsing the Matt Busby-led British side who could only finish third.

Raynor combined the national team duties with a management career in the Swedish domestic league before masterminding an incredible performance in the 1950 World Cup finals where his side reached the semi-finals before falling to eventual champions Uruguay. He took

Sweden to Olympic success once more, in 1952, as his team secured a bronze medal.

Raynor followed this achievement with spells at Juventus and Lazio before returning home for a brief spell at Coventry. He once again returned to take charge of Sweden and took his new side to the 1958 World Cup finals with the incredible achievements of 1950 still fresh in the mind. Amazingly, Raynor's side were once again the tournament's surprise package and finished runners-up behind a Pele-inspired Brazil, eventually losing the final despite taking an early lead.

In spite of his vast achievements Raynor never received the recognition he deserved in England and when he took over at Belle Vue it was following several years away from the game. Although the statistics indicate just another manager with an average record in charge at Doncaster Rovers, history shows that George Raynor may in fact have been the most talented name on the list.

FROM START TO FINISH

The first day of any season is always special. 'Anything can happen', 'Everyone starts equal', are just a couple of the clichés which are trotted out every August, but after those first 90 minutes are complete the trend is set and, rightly or wrongly, we prepare ourselves for a long, hard battle or a promotion push based on those opening-day results.

A look at the statistics shows that of the 9 promotions the Rovers have won in the Football League, 6 of them started off with an opening-day win. Similarly, of the 9 relegations the club has suffered, 4 began with defeats, 4 with draws and only once in the club's history has the side won the first game and gone on to be relegated.

For the record, the club's total record for full seasons in the Football League (up to 2010/11) on the opening day is:

Pld	W	D	L	
79	24	23	32	Win ratio – 30.3 per cent

The club's record on the last day of the season is also:

Pld	W	D	L	
79	18	23	38	Win ratio – 22.8 per cent

Clearly if you like a bet, you'd be wise not to bet on the Rovers getting a result on the last day of the season (although in my experience, you'd be wise not to bet on the Rovers at all).

FA YOUTH CUP

The FA Youth Cup is generally considered to be the showcase for tomorrow's top talent. Golden generations of players which made up the hugely successful Manchester United, Liverpool, Leeds and West Ham squads of the 1990s and 2000s all graduated from the youth squads. The likes of Beckham, Giggs, Butt, Neville, Owen, Carragher, Kewell and Carrick all appeared for their clubs in the final of the Youth Cup. That such quality is the competition's hallmark gives even greater credit to the Doncaster Rovers class of 1988 who surprised everyone by battling through to the final. Only an Arsenal side of real quality prevented them from completing the competition's biggest upset, but defeat in the final was no shame against a side that included names such as David Hillier, Steve Morrow and Kevin Campbell who went on to win major honours with the Gunners.

The Rovers side included Rufus Brevett (went on to play top flight football with QPR, Fulham and West Ham), Mark Rankine (graduated to captain Rovers midfield before moving to higher level with Wolves, Preston and Sheffield United), Paul Raven (moved to West Brom for a decent fee), Steve Gaughan and Steve Raffell (who both became key members of the Rovers first team). In fact there were only four members of the team which finished runners-up in the final who failed to play for the Rovers in the Football League. It was probably the success of the youth set-up at the time, masterminded by coach Steve Beaglehole (who himself went on to manage the full side) which prevented the club sliding into extinction. The talent coming through proved the club's only asset to offset the financial problems it faced. If it had managed to keep such a talented group together, who knows . . . ?

ME OLD FLOWER

It took Charlie Williams some time to become established in the first team, but by 1955 he was a key member of the Rovers side. He went on to make over 150 league appearance for the Rovers in a time when the colour of his skin was as stark an issue as the quality of his play. It is testament to his character that Williams, born and raised in Barnsley, never made an issue of the sometimes less-than-even-handed treatment he received from the media or the visiting fans.

It was when his time with Rovers ended that he found recognition on a national stage, as a short career as a singer blossomed into one as a comedian. The large framed, cheerful black man whose accent and outlook on life were unmistakably born in Yorkshire, proved the perfect comedy foil and helped provide the catchphrase 'eh up me old flower' which would become his trademark. Williams appeared regularly on TV's *The Comedians* and even hosted game show *The Golden Shot*. His television appearances were numerous during the 1970s and he even featured on *This Is Your Life* and published a book about his own life. He was appointed an MBE in 1999 and a year later was given a lifetime achievement award at the black comedy awards. In 2004, two years before his death, he was voted as the Rovers' all time cult hero proving that he will always cut an unmistakable and much-loved figure.

GREATEST GAMES

Rovers 4–3 Mansfield, 22 February 1975
The summer of 1974 brought at least a little optimism about the forthcoming Division Four campaign. However, a promising start soon gave way to a disappointing middle and the side slipped to second from bottom and were seemingly in free-fall. It was defensive frailties which had been the cause for most concern during the season and these shortcomings were to be sternly put to the test as league leaders Mansfield were the visitors to Belle Vue on 22 February 1975.

Any confidence Rovers had took a robust early blow as within seconds Mansfield forced a corner, and Rovers defenders Uzelac and Brookes could only watch as the ball bypassed everyone on its way to Colin Foster, who gleefully slammed the ball home with exactly 50 seconds of the contest gone.

Rovers began to scrap and fight and though the visitors' midfield was seeing a lot of the ball, Rovers battled on and gradually got back into proceedings, with Kitchen going close to an equaliser. Later, following a superb run down the flank from Curran, O'Callaghan's header towards goal was scrambled to safety.

The game was still finely poised but as the visitors poured forward the signs were looking ominous and the pressure told 6 minutes before the break. Two Mansfield efforts were blocked in quick succession before the ball broke to forward Terry Eccles who crashed the ball into the net, via the upright, to finally beat Brown and put Town two up.

Rovers still refused to lie down and looked to go direct towards the height and strength of Brendan O'Callaghan. As the ball was tossed into the penalty area O'Callaghan challenged Arnold and his punch fell to the feet of Steve Uzelac, who stabbed the ball home to get Rovers back into the game at half time.

Rovers came out for the second half clearly galvanised by Uzelac's late goal and the match developed into a real end-to-end encounter. On 59 minutes Ternent clipped a free kick from inside the Rovers' half in towards O'Callaghan who won another aerial battle to flick the ball forward to Peter Kitchen to latch onto, turn in and blast past the outstretched Arnold.

Rovers' prize pairing had the side level and now with the bit between their teeth, they began to surge forward, winning a free kick which was whipped into the box. With all eyes on the battle between O'Callaghan and Bird, Terry Curran made a great run undetected to the back post to hammer Rovers in front for the first time having fought back from 2–0 down.

Mansfield certainly weren't done yet and piled forwards. The pressure began to grow, and a loose ball broke to Eccles who drilled powerfully at goal. Despite Brown getting a hand on his drive, the ball found the back of the net and the league leaders were level late.

Rovers dug deep with Curran continually driving the team forward. Into the 88th minute, and with time running out, O'Callaghan again won a header and diverted the ball into the path of strike partner Peter Kitchen inside the box who, typically, in one slick movement, flashed home a difficult right-footed shot past the onrushing keeper to complete a remarkable never-say-die fightback. Curran had run himself into the ground, Kitchen had grabbed two characteristically clinical goals and O'Callaghan had been simply brilliant in the air as the side completed an astonishing and breathless 4–3 win.

PLAYING THE LONG GAME

The 1945/46 season saw the nation's footballing structure still adjusting to the end of the Second World War. With a full fixture list still not in place, the FA Cup was reintroduced and supplemented with the addition of the Third Division North Cup. Having topped their six-team qualification play-off, Rovers lined up for the first round proper against Stockport County. The first of the two legs was played at Belle Vue and ended in a 2–2 stalemate. The second leg at Stockport was also too close to call, and once again the teams were inseparable at 2–2, making it 4–4 on aggregate. The rules of the competition dictated extra time should be played, and if the scores were still level at its conclusion then the teams should simply play on until someone found the back of the net.

With the teams so closely matched, extra time came and went without a winner and the teams were forced to play on. The game went on and on and on before, with light fading fast and players and officials collapsing through exhaustion, eventually common sense prevailed and the contest was brought to an end after an incredible 3 hours and 25 minutes!

Three of the Rovers players were said to have worked a night shift the evening before, so it is unsurprising that on hearing the final whistle many of the players only had the energy to hobble off the pitch. Legend has it that some of the crowd had time to go home for their tea before returning to see the rest of the game! The incredible afternoon set a new record and still stands as the longest football match ever played.

Incidentally, the two clubs were forced to meet again in a replay, which Rovers won 4–0 with Ralph Maddison grabbing a hat-trick!

TOP CUP RUNS

Football League Trophy 2006/07

Rovers could have been given an easier route in the Johnstone's Paint-sponsored Football League Trophy in 2006/07. Instead, they managed to win difficult ties away at Huddersfield and Hartlepool, before seeing off Accrington at Belle Vue and then Darlington at their new Keepmoat Stadium home, which left them in the northern area final. The first leg was at Crewe's Gresty Road and turned out to be a belter. Rovers raced into a 2–0 half-time lead and looked to be cruising before the home side struck back with two goals of their own in a blistering start to the second period. Paul Heffernan added a third as Rovers looked to go into the second leg with an advantage but Luke Varney netted a late equaliser and the teams ended all square at 3–3.

The second leg was much anticipated and attracted a lot of media interest, including the Sky TV cameras, but it was

Crewe who looked set to spoil the party. Two goals in 4 first-half minutes gave them a comfortable lead at half time and looked to have sent them through to the final; but as in the first leg, it was the home side which came out galvanised. Heffernan got the Rovers back into the tie with a goal just past the hour but with only 7 minutes remaining they looked to be on their way out, before an infringement in the box handed them a lifeline. Up stepped Heffernan and sent the keeper the wrong way, only for further drama as the referee ordered a retake of the penalty because of players encroaching! Once again, up stepped 'Heffs' who fired the ball into the top right-hand corner of the net.

The Keepmoat was rocking now and the Rovers surged forward looking to capitalise. When the ball appeared at the feet of striker Jason Price, only a few yards from goal, the whole stadium held its breath. Price lashed at the ball, almost totally missing it, but his miskick only served to wrongfoot the defender and, at the second attempt he smashed the ball home to end a nail-biting, pulsating cup tie which ended 6–5 to the Rovers. It sent them to the Millennium Stadium, Cardiff, for the club's first ever major cup final.

Over 20,000 supporters from South Yorkshire made the trip to Wales but any who were late missed a dramatic start to the final against Bristol Rovers. Doncaster raced into a 2-goal lead within 5 minutes thanks to goals from Jonathan Forte and a fine finish from Paul Heffernan, but from then on struggled to settle and never really looked comfortable. Back came Bristol Rovers in the second period with a disputed penalty and some poor Rovers defending giving them a way back and sent the final into extra time.

It looked as though penalties would be required to settle the competition. However, with only 10 minutes of extra time remaining, skipper Graeme Lee stole a yard of space in the box and headed a winner. Everyone in red and white went ballistic at the final whistle with Lee collecting the trophy amid a backdrop of fireworks and celebrations. Rovers deservedly provided the perfect end to a special day.

First Round, 17 October 2006
Huddersfield Town   1–2   Doncaster Rovers
                                Price
                                Guy
Rovers: Filan, McDaid, Lee, S. Roberts, Streete, Griffith, Lockwood, Thornton, Price, Heffernan, Guy. Subs: Green for Streete, G. Roberts for Griffith.
Attendance: 3,629

Second Round, 30 October 2006
Hartlepool Untied   1–3   Doncaster Rovers
                                Heffernan (2)
                                Price
Rovers: Smith, Streete, G. Roberts, S. Roberts, Lockwood, Thornton, Griffith, Green, Heffernan, McCammon, Forte. Subs: Lee for Streete, Stock for Griffith, Price for Forte.
Attendance: 1,853

Third Round, 28 November 2006
Doncaster Rovers   2–0   Accrington Stanley
Heffernan
Thornton
Rovers: Smith, Streete, G. Roberts, Lockwood, Lee, Thornton, Coppinger, Forte, Heffernan, McCammon, McDaid. Subs: Green for Lockwood, Guy for Forte, Wilson for McDaid.
Attendance: 3,209

Northern Semi-Final, 9 January 2007
Doncaster Rovers   2–0   Darlington
Heffernan
Price

Rovers: Smith, Lockwood, Gilbert, Thornton, S. Roberts, Stock, Dyer, Green, Heffernan, Guy, Price. Subs: Pittman for Gilbert, Coppinger for Dyer, Wilson for Guy.
Attendance: 8,009

Northern Final first leg, 30 January 2007

Crewe Alexandra   3–3   Doncaster Rovers
Heffernan (2, inc 1 pen)
Stock

Rovers: Smith, O'Connor, G. Roberts, S. Roberts, Lee, Stock, Guy, Wilson, Heffernan, McCammon, Price. Subs: Lockwood for McCammon, Green for Price.
Attendance: 4,631

Northern Final second leg, 12 February 2007

Doncaster Rovers   3–2   Crewe Alexandra
Heffernan (2, inc 1 pen)
Price

Rovers: Smith, Lockwood, G. Roberts, S. Roberts, Lee, Stock, Coppinger, Wilson, Heffernan, Price, O'Connor. Subs: Nelthorpe for S. Roberts, Thornton for Stock, Green for G. Roberts.
Attendance: 12,561

Final, 1 April 2007

(at the Millennium Stadium, Cardiff)
Doncaster Rovers   3–2   Bristol Rovers
Forte
Heffernan
Lee

Rovers: Sullivan, O'Connor, McDaid, Lockwood, Lee, Stock, Coppinger, Green, Heffernan, Price, Forte. Subs: Wilson for Stock, Thornton for Price, Guy for Forte.
Attendance: 59,024

CRAMB KEEPS OUT CHESTER

On 8 February 1997 the Rovers were on the wrong end of a thumping at the hands of Chester City. Things had gone from bad to worse at the Deva Stadium as 2–0 down at half time quickly became 4–0. With only minutes remaining and the score having reached 6–0, keeper Dean Williams was penalised following a foul in the box. The Rovers number 1 was sent off with the score already at 6–0 and the home side having been awarded a penalty.

More at home doing his work in the opposition box, striker and leading goalscorer Colin Cramb was forced to take over duties between the sticks. Cramb pulled on the gloves and promptly saved the resulting penalty before going on to keep a clean sheet for the remaining moments of the game!

A TOUGH DAY AT THE SEASIDE

Rovers won the Conference Trophy in 1999 and in doing so provided a day that signalled the club had returned from the brink of oblivion. However, things could have been different.

In the semi-final that year, the Rovers travelled to the holders, a talented Morecambe side, for a game which turned out to be quite eventful. Rovers enjoyed a bright first half and led 2–0 at the break thanks to goals from Ian Duerden. The second half saw Shaun Goodwin forced off with injury, Colin Sutherland (whose wrist was already in plaster) was forced to play on with a shoulder injury, and midfielder Jason Minett was sent off.

Things got even worse for the Rovers as the referee awarded the home side a penalty, only for Rovers keeper Andy Woods to make a superb save to keep his team ahead. The referee seemed inclined to find Morecambe a way back into the game and moments later awarded them a second penalty. Amazingly, Woods made another great save and the Rovers held on for 2–1 win with all the plaudits rightly going to Woods for incredibly saving two penalties in the same game!

COMPLETE LEAGUE RECORD

Season	Competition	Final pos	average attendance
1890/91	Midland League	2	Unknown
1891/92	Midland League	6	Unknown
1892/93	Midland League	5	Unknown
1893/94	Midland League	8	Unknown
1894/95	Midland League	12	Unknown
1895/96	Midland League	10	Unknown
1896/97	Midland League	1	Unknown
1897/98	Midland League	10	Unknown
1898/99	Midland League	1	Unknown
1899/1900	Midland League	7	Unknown
1900/01	Midland League	2	Unknown
1901/02	Division 2	7	4,000 approx.
1902/03	Division 2	16	5,800 approx.
1903/04	Midland League	11	Unknown
1904/05	Division 2	18	3,000 approx.
1905/06	Midland League	14	Unknown
1906/07	Midland League	17	Unknown
1907/08	Midland League	15	Unknown
1908/09	Midland League	11	Unknown
1909/10	Midland League	14	Unknown
1910/11	Midland League	3	Unknown

Season	Competition	Final pos	average attendance
1911/12	Midland League	3	Unknown
1912/13	Midland League	4	Unknown
1913/14	Midland League	16	Unknown
1914/15	Midland League	15	Unknown
1915/16	Midland Comb	7	Unknown
NO LEAGUE FOOTBALL OWING TO FIRST WORLD WAR			
1920/21	Midland League	16	Unknown
1921/22	Midland League	13	Unknown
1922/23	Midland League	2	Unknown
1923/24	Division 3 North	9	7,285
1924/25	Division 3 North	18	5,380
1925/26	Division 3 North	10	5,190
1926/27	Division 3 North	8	5,334
1927/28	Division 3 North	4	7,574
1928/29	Division 3 North	5	6,733
1929/30	Division 3 North	14	4,652
1930/31	Division 3 North	15	4,176
1931/32	Division 3 North	15	3,903
1932/33	Division 3 North	6	5,262
1933/34	Division 3 North	5	6,000
1934/35	Division 3 North	1	10,761
1935/36	Division 2	18	14,122
1936/37	Division 2	22	11,697
1937/38	Division 3 North	2	12,373
1938/39	Division 3 North	2	11,587
NO LEAGUE FOOTBALL OWING TO SECOND WORLD WAR			
1946/47	Division 3 North	1	15,339
1947/48	Division 2	21	22,261
1948/49	Division 3 North	3	13,284
1949/50	Division 3 North	1	17,901
1950/51	Division 2	11	22,799
1951/52	Division 2	16	21,066
1952/53	Division 2	13	15,324

Season	Competition	Final pos	average attendance
1953/54	Division 2	12	16,919
1954/55	Division 2	18	12,236
1955/56	Division 2	17	12,420
1956/57	Division 2	14	12,389
1957/58	Division 2	22	11,132
1958/59	Division 3	22	6,652
1959/60	Division 4	17	5,251
1960/61	Division 4	11	4,754
1961/62	Division 4	21	4,470
1962/63	Division 4	16	6,305
1963/64	Division 4	14	6,360
1964/65	Division 4	9	8,557
1965/66	Division 4	1	10,594
1966/67	Division 3	23	7,908
1967/68	Division 4	10	7,852
1968/69	Division 4	1	10,212
1969/70	Division 3	11	8,561
1970/71	Division 3	23	4,479
1971/72	Division 4	12	4,126
1972/73	Division 4	17	2,258
1973/74	Division 4	22	3,072
1974/75	Division 4	17	2,975
1975/76	Division 4	10	6,083
1976/77	Division 4	8	4,500
1977/78	Division 4	12	3,228
1978/79	Division 4	22	3,072
1979/80	Division 4	12	4,403
1980/81	Division 4	3	5,411
1981/82	Division 3	19	5,263
1982/83	Division 3	23	3,004
1983/84	Division 4	2	3,729
1984/85	Division 3	14	4,103
1985/86	Division 3	11	2,822

Season	Competition	Final pos	average attendance
1986/87	Division 3	13	2,402
1987/88	Division 3	24	1,893
1988/89	Division 4	23	2,166
1989/90	Division 4	20	2,710
1990/91	Division 4	11	2,835
1991/92	Division 4	21	2,058
1992/93	Division 4	16	2,411
1993/94	Division 3	15	2,478
1994/95	Division 3	9	2,585
1995/96	Division 3	13	2,090
1996/97	Division 3	19	2,091
1997/98	Division 3	24	1,715
1998/99	Conference	16	3,380
1999/2000	Conference	12	2,981
2000/01	Conference	9	2,281
2001/02	Conference	4	2,409
2002/03	Conference	3	3,540
2003/04	Division 3	1	6,939
2004/05	League One	10	6,886
2005/06	League One	8	6,139
2006/07	League One	11	7,746
2007/08	League One	3	7,978
2008/09	Championship	14	11,964
2009/10	Championship	12	10,991
2010/11	Championship	21	10,258

DONCASTER ROVERS – KEY MOMENTS

1879	Club formed and began playing friendly and exhibition games
1891/92	Joined Midland League
1896/97	Midland League champions
1897/98	Also played in Yorkshire League
1898/99	Midland League champions for the second time
1900/01	Midland League runners-up
1901	Elected to Football League Division Two
1903	Failed to be re-elected to Division Two, rejoined Midland League
1904/05	Elected back into Football League Division Two
1905	Failed to be re-elected to Division Two, rejoined Midland League
1919	Did not re-join Midland League immediately after First World War
1920/21	Rejoined Midland League
1922/23	Midland League runners-up
1923/24	Elected back into Football League Division Three North
1934/35	Football League Division Three North champions, promoted to Division Two
1937	Relegated to Division Three North
1937/38	Football League Division Three North runners-up
1938/39	Football League Division Three North runners-up
1946	Jackie Bestall appointed manager
1946/47	Football League Division Three North champions, promoted to Division Two
1948	Relegated to Division Three North
1949	Peter Doherty appointed manager
1949/50	Football League Division Three North champions, promoted to Division Two

1954	Alick Jeffrey makes Rovers debut
1958	Relegated to Division Three
1959	Relegated to Division Four
1965/66	Football League Division Four champions (on goal average), promoted to Division Three
1967	Relegated to Division Four
1968/69	Football League Division Four champions, promoted to Division Three
1971	Relegated to Division Four
1978	Billy Bremner appointed manager
1980/81	Promoted to Division Three
1983	Relegated to Division Four
1983/84	Football League Division Four runners-up, promoted to Division Three
1988	Relegated to Division Four
1993	Club taken over by Dinard Trading – Ken Richardson
1998	Relegated to Conference
1998	John Ryan purchases club
1999	Won Conference Trophy
2000	Retained Conference Trophy
2001	Dave Penney appointed manager
2002/03	Won Conference play-off final and promoted back into the Football League
2003/04	Football League Division Three champions, promoted to League One
2006	Sean O'Driscoll appointed manager
2007	Club won first ever major trophy – the Football League Trophy at Cardiff's Millennium Stadium
2007/08	Finished third in League One and won play-off final in club's first ever appearance at Wcmbley, winning promotion to the Championship and return to English football's second tier for first time in over 50 years

JOHN RYAN

'When I first started watching the club forty years ago they were in the Second Division. I would love to see us back at that level.' Thus spoke John Ryan in 1999 following his official takeover of Doncaster Rovers. No one would have believed it possible, but Ryan was true to his word achieving that goal and so much more, in less than a decade. Ryan bought Doncaster Rovers for £50,000 and he says, 'I was done, it wasn't worth anywhere near that.' He made four promises: to return Rovers to the league; to secure them a new ground; to take them to a major cup final and to restore them to the second tier.

'Let's be honest, people thought I was completely off my head,' he says.

RYAN SAYS

'When I became chairman we were in such a bad financial state that we had no players, no balls and no nets. We've come so far since then; I doubt any other club has been on quite our sort of journey.'

John Ryan on the size of the task waiting for him

'I call the strip outside the ground Miami. It reminds me of the real Miami.'

John Ryan with rose-tinted glasses on Rovers' new lakeside home

'It's these moments when we play in the Millennium [Stadium] average fans say, that's Doncaster Rovers, what's going on!?'

Ryan on seeing Doncaster being successful